CAROL MALONE SISKOVIC

LOOKING FORWARD LOOKING BACK

Looking Forward Looking Back

An Autobiography including Poems

Carol M. Siskovic

Basking Turtle Publishing
San Antonio, Texas

ISBN- (Amazon Print) 979-8-9922344-0-4
ISBN- (ebook) 979-8-9922344-1-1

Basking Turtle Publishing
San Antonio, Texas

Printed in the United States of America

Table of Contents

Introduction

There come many times in life when you find yourself looking both ways - forward and back. During youth, it seems always to be the forward look. As one grows older, the tendency becomes to sooth oneself with memories - millions of memories. We tend to lounge and lull in the really good ones. But we also find ourselves returning to those strategic times that were painful, but also so powerful in determining who and what we became. One begins to emphasize "first" and "last." The first dream, the first kiss, the first love, the first job, the first goal, the first terrible loss. So many firsts. And, of course, many of those are lost one way or another. What we find, through the years, is that if we are fortunate…the firsts and lasts somehow balance themselves out and turn us into what we hope will be considered a decent human being who has managed to make a positive difference in the world.

So often in history, the precious and helpful stories of a life are not passed on; if they are, for a while, they frequently become lost forever in the unending swirl of Time. Present generations can learn from the past, but so many many stories sink forever into the sands of History's ocean floor. Our only hope to save ourselves and our personal stories is in recording them through written, spoken or pictured means. With our writings, our photographs, our videos, we can leave some record of our lives, our thoughts, our values, our hopes and dreams, the difficulties and despairs we overcame and hopefully grew from, experiences that formed us, and our unending loves that we hope will endure beyond death.

With hope, we leave behind what we can of ourselves, our memories and thoughts, for anyone, especially loved ones and family, who may benefit in some way from OUR words and records.

Landscapes Without, Within

What surrounds, what abounds,
can affect, build, often control.
Stars, skyscrapers, trees, mosquitoes, minnows,
all forms, lifeforms, and yes, hope, that "thing with feathers"
move us forward, onward, into, onto the "next."

But…. our fear of the everlasting exception,
our intellectual need to assert blame or cause.
keep us hesitant and questioning,
weakened by circumstances chosen or unchosen.

Or sometimes strengthened. We look,
often stare, never quite sure, seeking certainty
from sunrise brightness through smog 'til sunset,
through rotation, forever searching, finding, losing.

Though looking and truly seeing,
we may still be blinded, may even choose unseeing.
But…even when blinded in mysterious ways,
our inner landscapes and memories
can still inspire, uplift, sustain.

Summation of lives, desires, disappointments,
written perhaps in the constance and variety within
our ever-shifting or never-changing landscapes,
forever vibrate with eternal possibility and regeneration.
We capture what we can to inspire all we can.

Carol M. Siskovic

Stop! Look! See! Remember!

Look at these hands,
the years reflected there,
the soft strokes, the hard scars.
the revealing lines, impressions
of all I've touched.

Look at this body,
a little shorter now, saggier,
farther from the perfection once sought,
closer to a perfection of sorts.
It has lasted, I give it that.
And when it finally resigns,
I'd like it labeled "Well Used,"
certainly not "Nearly New."
I want my money"s worth!

Look at this hair.
It may last longer than bones,
but for now I can control it better than
my squeaking, creaking joints.
Some say hair will grow past death.
It may end up in a bird's nest,
in a stuffed pillow or an old scrapbook,
or simply floating in the mythic winds.

Look at this face and neck. The folds and dunes
can hypnotize like a shifting landscape
in some ancient desert.

Look at these eyes. Same unchanging color,
but the shades have dropped,
and the bags are packed.
They've seen so much more than I dreamed,
so much less than I hoped.
Even when they close, they see…
even when they sleep.
But they will never see enough
though I may say otherwise.

Look at these lips. The tongue quickly
moistens them, still anticipating a kiss,
many kisses, all kinds of kisses.
Thinner lips, slightly engraved,
but caressing the same voice,
toned deeper and wiser, perhaps,
but the same.

Look. Look at me. Look at us.
The present. The past. The possible.
Look at us this moment. This moment!
Single diamonds shimmering on the string of Life!
Treasured jewels. Works of art. Sweet riches untold.
"Such a lovely, unforgettable sight!"

Carol M. Siskovic

Beginnings

1

My name is Frances Carol Malone Siskovic. For a long time I had no idea why those two first names were chosen, or by whom, but eventually my mother informed me that my Dad had chosen one and the other was picked by his older sister, my Aunt Curt. She said that since Aunt Curt had crocheted an entire baby outfit for the new baby including top, bottom, coat, booties, hat, and gloves that she was allowed to pick a name. At the time Mother could not remember which name was selected by which person since they came up with the names and the order together. It was common in those days to call a child by the second, less formal, name, so I suspect that my Dad chose Carol, the name I have always been called by. Years later, when social security and other government records became so important, people were called by their first names formally. That has proven a problem for me in my retirement years so I have had to switch to using my full name of Frances Carol Malone Siskovic.

I was born on a Saturday, April 29, 1939, outside a little town called Dublin, Mississippi, in a sharecropper's house in a neighborhood called Cagle's Crossroads, or Cagle's Crossing. For a long time, I didn't know a lot about the families and area I came from, but eventually I did learn the following facts:

There was a family living there in the "Delta," northwestern Mississippi cotton country, by the name of Cagle. Hodge and Hazel Cagle, and Hodge's mother, Granny Cagle, were considered to be part of the original family of the community. Granny was at every church function, and everybody listened to what she had to say. She lived with my best friend, Murlyn Spurry, and Murlyn's parents, Murl and Mary Spurry. Mary Spurry was one of Granny Cagle's daughters. The story of the origin of Cagle's Crossing as I remember is that when the community was still pretty much unsettled, a man named Cagle began to farm the area. He had a wife and five children. When the wife died, he was in such need of someone to help with everything that he sent back a message to what was called "the Hills," from which he had come. He wrote that he needed a bride, and would somebody please find one for him and bring her to him with a preacher.

The story is that sometime later a young woman was brought by mule and wagon and that she became Mrs. Cagle and immediate mother of five. She then proceeded to supply Mr. Cagle with five more children. So the community became known as Cagle's Crossroads because two dirt roads ran into and out of the area and crossed at that point. Eventually, a community church and a country store were established on the northwestern corner. I don't know exactly when or how it happened, but that country store at Cagle's Crossing was later owned and run during my early years by my grandfather, William Eddie Malone. It was later sold to a Mr. and Mrs. J. R. Sally whose daughter, Lucy Jean, became a friend of mine. The church is still there as of 2024, but the store, once a community gathering point, is no more. In the southeastern corner of this place where two dirt roads crossed, I was born, April 29, 1939, in a sharecropper house surrounded by cotton.

Dogwalk Road ran from the little town of Dublin to Cagle's Crossroads. Joining roads were first dirt, then graveled, then later blacktopped, widened, and better maintained. Just west of the store was Union Chapel where people of all religions in the community came to worship. All the years I was growing up, they alternated preachers from the various Protestant churches around. When people joined the church, they had to declare which one they were joining. My dad and brothers chose the Baptist. My mother and sister joined the Methodist. And when I joined, I chose Baptist, but after we moved away, I became a Methodist at Minter City Methodist Church. Both of those churches were still standing and active when I visited in October, 2023.

Cagle's Crossing Church was pretty well known throughout the area for its all-day singings and its community get-togethers with trailers pulled in a circle under shady trees and piled with homemade covered dishes to share. Some of my best early memories were under those trees choosing the yummiest desserts and listening to the music from the church.

Community life and family life were very important as I grew up and obviously gave me the desire for closeness and connection as a natural part of a good life. On my mother's side, we had the Hortons, the Ramays, and the McCulloughs, and on my father's side, the Malones and the Vanlandinghams. Their families had all come from Europe, and they came, of course, for a better life.

As I understood it, on both sides, they had people who went into indenture to be able to seek a chance for a new life. People who had no resources often made agreements of indenture for seven years, agreeing to work for an individual as repayment for being provided passage to that person's place, and for their minimal support during the seven years. In order to get a chance in a new country, they were willingly under the control of the person who supported them for the seven year indentureship. After indenture, new settlers, in the South especially, often became sharecroppers, making an agreement to plant, tend, and harvest a piece of land, usually about 20 or 40 acres. At the harvest, profits were shared according to how much aide the sharecropper had needed before harvest. The small farm houses provided were called sharecropper houses. They were called shotgun houses if you could stand at the front and shoot through the front and back door of the one or two rooms without damaging anything. They were called dogtrot houses if two shotgun styles were joined with a covered walkway from front to back which provided protection for dogs and other animals. This inexpensive housing could be seen all over the Mississippi Delta when I was growing up. A common sight wherever you drove were fields full of workers, usually chopping or picking cotton, and scattered almost everywhere, many many sharecropper houses. On my last visit in 2023, all of that was gone, the fields now planted and harvested by modern machinery. The house I was born in and the three other houses I lived in at the Cagle's Crossroads area no longer existed. Part of one had remained in 2022, but was now gone.

In my adulthood, I learned from my Uncle Sammy (mother's youngest brother), who in his last years had done a lot of research, that my relatives on the McCullough side and the Horton side definitely fought in the Revolutionary War. I assume the Malone's did too, but I never got any assurance of that. I also assume some fought in the War Between the States. On the Malone side, they did extremely well, eventually, and had a plantation house, or very nice farmhouse, that burned, which was extremely discouraging to all of them. There was a story of an unsuccessful bucket brigade. Another story was that, supposedly, a Jerry Malone, possibly my great grandfather, worked in a cotton gin where he lost an arm by getting it caught in the machinery somehow. On the Horton side, they never did manage to accumulate any wealth, but they always farmed land as sharecroppers, and, eventually, some owned small farms.

My mother's father, William Henry (Will) Horton, and her mother, Emma Belle Ramay Horton, married at a young age and eventually produced a total of ten kids and numerous grandchildren. My mother's sister, Aunt May, was the first one born to the family. Next came my mother. Since my mother was a second girl, her father thought that he might not have any boys, so he wanted to make sure he had a kid named after him. They named her Willie Blanche, a name she always hated. Out of the ten children they eventually produced, nine made it to adulthood. The oldest, May, suffered from polio as a child, which resulted in stunted growth and being crippled. She did live into her sixties, but was handicapped most of her life and waddled rather than walked.

Needless to say, my mother as the healthiest of the older children became a very young babysitter and helpmate for her mother. Her mother's brother, "Uncle Johnny," took pride in coming up with nicknames for the children. Zella May was always known as "Baby," and my mother became "Buntsy," but as she grew older, married, and had children of her own, no one ever called her that anymore. I later found it fascinating that when she was old and developed dementia, Buntsy sort of came back in her head, and she became a little girl again in many ways. I've often said that I would write Buntsy's story. I did write a poem, "When Buntsy Was A Baby," when participating in a summer writing project seminar in 1985. One story that I love is about one of the many times my mother ran away when she was old and living with my sister, Jean. After Jean found her and brought her home, she sat her down in the kitchen, then kneeled in front of her, holding her hands. She asked, "Mother, why do you keep running away? I get so worried, afraid I might not find you." Then, Mother answered, "I want to go home. I miss my mother…." Then Jean asked, "Well, why can't I be your mother? Can I? Can I be your mother?" She said Mother looked at her hard, and then slowly said, "Well…okay…." After that, she calmed down a bit, and things got easier for a while. Obviously, even in old age, even with dementia, parental importance does not diminish.

After two girls, Emma and Will proceeded to have boys. They had Dudley and then they had William Norris (called Bill Jack) and Roy Claude. Somewhere in there, they had a little girl named Betsy who caught diptheria and died when very young - a deep sadness to May and my mother, Blanche, who had taken care of her. Next, they had Leora Eileen, called Doad all her life. She was my Aunt Doad, the mother of my cousin Gerald Cooper who was like a little brother to me. Then they had Thomas Ray who was called Bijah. Next, they had Winky, Uncle Winky, to me, whose name was Charles Wayne. Then Samuel Eural, and he was called either Eural, Sammy, or Sambo all his life. That was my mother's side - always a big and close family. In fact, a yearly Horton family reunion has been held for many years by Gerald Cooper at his church outside Hernando, Mississippi.

Both sides of my family grew up in relatively the same area in Northeast Mississippi, from Lovejoy, Water Valley, Calhoun City, and nearby communities, ofter referred to as "The Hills," but my family ended up in the flatland at the edge of the hills called "cotton country," the Mississippi Delta. Cotton was the money crop; nearly everything else was "food crops."

On the Malone side, my father's sister Curtis Mabel, Aunt Curt Sherman, was the eldest, and then came my father, Thomas Seabron Malone. Seabron is an Irish name, as is Malone, which is interesting because the fact that we were of Irish descent was something I did not know until I was in college and suddenly realized that most of the people in my family had typically Irish names. For all I know, the

"Molly Malone" in the well-known song may have been an ancestor. At least I like to think so. But no one in the family ever talked of anything Irish. I didn't even know that the little town where my siblings and I went to school, Dublin, was the name of a major city in Ireland. Many years later when my husband was stationed in England, Joel and I traveled to Ireland. Our first night in Dublin, as we entered a downtown Pub, Joel cried out, "My wife was born in Dublin, and now she's come home!" It was almost a unanimous cry of "Welcome home, dearie!" People wanted to buy us drinks all evening long. I wish I could say we felt bad for the deception, but we didn't. It was just too much fun. Besides, nobody ever asked those nutty Americans any questions!

In my Dad's "Irish" family came four more sisters and one brother. Aunt Curt had married a Baptist preacher and had two boys and two girls. After Daddy, the second child came, Clara Waldrop, who died at middle age of a stroke, leaving five children. After her, came Daddy's only brother, James Franklin, my Uncle Jim Frank Malone who had a girl, Martha Jane, and a boy, Jeff. Martha Jane, my frequent childhood playmate, got cancer and died at age 47. Last in Daddy's family were his three younger sisters - Aunt Flossie Waldrop (she and Clara married brothers), Aunt Trudy Davis, and Aunt Mary Nell Hardy. That was seven families, all with cousins who became lifetime friends. They pretty much made for a crowd at Malone family reunions, at first held at various homes, then eventually occurring every October at the Waldrop family Sardis Lake cabin. At the 2023 reunion, it was announced that the name was now changed from the Malone reunion to the Waldrop and Cousins Reunion. It seems we no longer have very many attending with the last name of Malone. However, one of Roy and Flossie Waldrop's descendants, a little boy, was given the first name of Malone.

The Malone family for many years got together at every major holiday and many times in between. The Hortons did also but less often. When I was growing up, reunions were a common thing - our main entertainment that we looked forward to. The families would usually meet on Sundays and holidays, and every family would take some food. It would be a big picnic, the men all together talking, the women all together and keeping things in order, and the kids all playing together, nearly always outside, unless the weather wouldn't permit it. All of my growing up years were years of family on both sides, but the two families hardly ever merged or got together. They had met each other, and they knew each other by names just from conversations. But as far as having reunions together, we didn't. They were always separately done.

My mother and dad had met at a community church in northwest Mississippi called LoveJoy Church, which is still there, and open to the public. I have visited there a number of times, and the doors were always unlocked I don't know if it was a union church or not, but it seemed to be a church that accepted anybody who wanted to go. My mother's family went there, and it was not far from their farmhouse. My dad sometimes went there, too. They usually had get-togethers on Sunday nights, which might be called youth parties, and my mother met him there. One Sunday, he asked her if he could pick her up to go with him the next Sunday, and she said yes. As she waited at her house to be picked up, a friend and the friend's boyfriend were waiting with her for Seab to come so they could travel together in a mule-pulled wagon or by just walking together. They waited and waited, and it was getting late, but my future dad had not come, so the three of them decided they would go without him. When they arrived, to their surprise and embarrassment, my dad was there with another girl! Of course, my mother was greatly disappointed and embarrassed, but she gave up on him and went on and had a good time.

Then, the next Sunday, he came up to her and said, "I know that I did wrong, but somebody else set it up for me, and I really would like to take you next time, and I promise you if you go with me, I will be sure and pick you up." My dad was eight years older than my mother. She was 18, considered "old enough" at that time. It was a "not-so-promising" start, but she was attracted to him, and I guess he was to her. The next Sunday, he actually did come and pick her up and they began to court.

Pretty soon, he asked her to marry him. It was around Christmas time, in 1924. My dad had been born in 1898, and my mother had been born in 1906. They married three days after Christmas on December 28, 1924. I always found it interesting, a bit odd and shocking, that on their wedding night they came from the church after being married, and spent their first night together in her parent's house.

It was just a sharecropper's house, but I believe there were at least four good-sized rooms in that house with a big walkway between the two halves so it was probably a dogtrot house. One room was a kitchen, and one room was a gathering room, maybe with beds. At least two of the rooms had a lot of beds in them, and they could put a bunch of family in them. They did, however, give my mother and dad a room alone for their wedding night. A schoolmate once told me that was not the case with her sister, as she had been in the same room, different bed, as her just-married sister!

The next morning, my future parents got up early and packed up the few things they'd been given. My mother always said she had three or four dresses: her good Sunday dress, her Saturday nice dress, and one or two everyday dresses, plus a lot of aprons. Her mom gave her a boiler and a skillet to cook with and a couple of household items that they could pack up and take with them. My mother's father, my grandfather, Will Horton, put them in a wagon and drove them to a little nearby train station. They caught the train there and went to Lake Cormorant in north Mississippi, where Daddy had arranged to sharecrop for the year of 1924. They arrived at their stop and then got a ride out to the piece of land where he was sharecropping. They spent their second night of marriage in a two-room shotgun house, their home for the first year of their marriage.

I did not know any of this until I was grown, when my mother and I, with my three children at the time, made the long drive from her home in Memphis, Tennessee, to my home, then in Bowie, Maryland. We had hours to share stories, probably a first experience for her, as none of my siblings remembered ever hearing any of them. I just wish I had asked so many more questions.

She told me how for twenty years, they share-cropped. That meant that every January, they had to make a new deal for where he would work. Share-cropping at that time was set up so that if you provided your own food and supplies needed, you could farm the land and get half the profits that came from the crops. But if the landowner provided you with a house to live in, food, and supplies, you would get a fourth of the profits. My parents moved frequently through the years, always trying to improve their situation. A few times they would return to a house they had lived in previously. She also told me that several times they had lost everything in house fires. Once, the story goes, my Dad was trying to rescue belongings before everything went up, so he grabbed a mattress and then started putting dishes in a tin washtub. But on rushing to get out, he got mixed up, and instead of tossing the mattress out the door and carrying the tub, he did the reverse and broke all the dishes! Needless to say, he never lived that down.

My oldest brother, Lorren Gwin, was born in Lake Cormorant. He was not their first child. I learned when grown that before Gwin, they had a baby boy who only lived seven days. Mother said she thought at the time that he had died because they were afraid to sleep with the baby, afraid they might smother him, and that he had gotten too cold in the dresser-drawer bed they put him in on the floor. Her mother, Mama Horton, also took the blame for his death as she had asked them to name the baby William Byron. Supposedly, she had pressed that name on two other boy babies that had not lived. I am not sure whose. With a third death, she said that name was surely cursed, and she would never allow anyone to use it again!

My sister Myra Jean was born in Jonestown, MS, almost two years after Gwin, and my brother Thomas Wade was born two years after her in Rena Laura, MS. Then, eight years later, after my parents had considered their family complete, I was born at Cagle's Crossroads.

I was born in the southeast corner of Cagle's Crossroads on a Saturday. I never learned if it was early or late in the day just before or after midnight. The story is that my boy cousins, J.H. Sherman and brothers Charles and J.W. Waldrop walked across the fields in the dark to sneak to an outside window to witness the birth of a baby. They had seen a lot of animals born, but never a human. Fortunately, or unfortunately, my dad caught them, threatened them with a resounding slap of his razor strap, and they went running across the fields back home. They told me this story for the first time at my mother's funeral when I was 47 years old.

Our local doctor, Dr. Ballard, who lived on Dogwalk Road, not far from Dublin, did not so much deliver babies as check them and the mothers after the birth. That was the case with my Mother at my birth. He was the one who sent in the papers for the birth certificates. I don't know whose fault it was for not checking properly, but I did not learn until I needed the certificate for college entrance that the name, Carol, which I had been called all my life, was missing from the certificate. On it, I was Frances Malone, no time of birth listed. It only took a simple letter requesting the change to get a revised birth certificate. I don't think it would be that easy in present times.

In January after I was born, my parents moved to a bigger nearby sharecropper's house that I later referred to as "the dredgeditch house" because it sat right next to a deeply dug ditch, often found in that area to provide drainage and a collecting place for rainwater. At that time, we had a dog named Scotty. It was a black and white spotted dog, and I loved him. The story goes that I would hold on to Scotty's back as I started to toddle around. That dog helped me learn to walk. Since then, I have always loved animals. I have no real memory of Scotty, just a picture of us together that feels like a memory, as described in my poem "Precious Memory."

Scotty was the beginning of many pets I had in the future, including one called Snowball when I was five years old. The new puppy wriggled from my arms one morning as I watched my siblings leave on the school bus. It ran beneath the bus wheels and became my first and extremely memorable experience with death. I blamed the bus driver for being in such a hurry and not stopping when he heard the first yelp. Many years later I wrote a poem about it entitled, "I still Hate You, Mr. Cagle." I later wrote another poem that was less resentful called "Elegiac Fever."

Pets became very important to me as I was growing up. There were always a number of dogs and cats on the farm, some more treasured than others. I especially remember my Collie dog, Jennie, who had to be taken to a vet appointment from which she did not return. Spot, Rusty, Missy, and Blackie were others. And there was our one horse, Dynamite, who dumped me a few times.

We also had a cat named Whitefoot who loved to scoot in through the back porch screen door every chance she got. Animals were never allowed in the house. Animals were supposed to stay outside either under the house or in other shelters but NEVER inside the home. That was low class! Whenever Whitefoot would sneak in, I got another cursing lesson from my mother. As the cat wound figure eights around her ankles while she tried to cook or clean, she would kick at it and exclaim, "Dang yo' hide!" And then, "Somebody get this cat outta here!" That "dang" cat lived for over fifteen years!

After the dredgeditch house, my parents moved to another sharecropping house over on a gravel road that I always called the Johnson-Muse road, because families with those names lived there for many years. My first real memory was of rolling on the kitchen floor of that house.

The January before I was five years old, in 1944, my mother and father had finally managed to make a down payment on a place of their own with about 360 acres of land. They referred to it as the "Powell Place" because that was the man who had owned it. The whole time I was growing up, I thought they had said "Pal Place," and I thought that was the best possible name for a new home and a new start. I was in college before I learned of my misunderstanding.

Even this new house that they actually bought didn't have plumbing or electricity at first. Out behind the house, there was a simple small framed building, an outdoor toilet, inside which a deep hole was dug. The toilet had to be moved a few yards every few years where they would dig a new hole. They always threw the dirt from the new hole into the old toilet hole to cover it up. You could tell where the toilet had been because the grass grew thick and green over that spot. That is also my first memory of a "two-seater," allowing two people to go at the same time.

In those years, we had to use a hand pump for house water; you would pump your own water right at the back porch from an in-ground well. There were some other pumps near the barn, but there were no water lines into the house until after a few successful farming years allowed them to afford the cost of indoor plumbing and electricity. Even then, for years we had to keep oil lamps and buckets of water handy for sudden, unexplained outages.

When they decided they could afford running water, my parents had to purchase an automatic pump that would bring water from a deep well via pipes that had been run under and into the house. They built a house around the pump, called the Pump House. It was a place where they stored other things too, including a salt bin for meats, but mainly it protected the water pump. When that was installed, we were able to have running water in the house complete with a kitchen sink, a bathroom sink, and a toilet that could flush.

Later on, they even installed a water heater in the hallway near the bathroom so that they could have hot water for the bath and the kitchen. Before that, we had to heat water on the stove for a hot bath. I remember taking baths in an aluminum tub placed on the kitchen floor, quite often with my cousin Gerald sitting on one rim while I sat across from him. We'd take turns dipping in the water. Other improvements we got with running water and electricity were a refrigerator, a chest freezer, and some electric fans. Also, they were able to install a gas line. We had butane gas heaters and a gas stove. That required having the gas man come once a month to refill our butane tank. My brother-in-law, Paul Broadway, worked at Texas Gas Company doing such work for many years.

Before those changes and after, we always had to be careful each night to extinguish all fires, then relight them on rising each morning. That was usually Daddy's job. In the winter we had to bundle under heavy covers. During warm and hot months, we always slept on the sleeping porch at the Pal Place, with the windows all wide open. With electricity, we also learned the pleasure and comfort of electric fans.

Although my parents, sister, and brothers lived without these luxuries that are just assumed as owed to everyone now-a-days, I only had to live a short time without them. But even this short time taught me to appreciate everything I had. It taught me to not waste anything and to not take anything for granted. Even after easy times, this lesson has stayed with me.

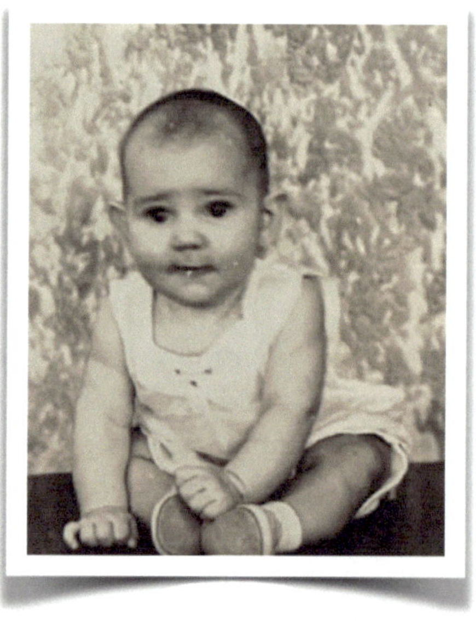

To get Carol to stop crying and smile, her Dad took his cigar out of his mouth and asked "Do ya wanna smoke?"

Cagle's Crossing and Union Chapel, 2024

A typical outhouse

Will Horton and Emma Belle
Ramay Horton
Maternal Grandparents

Big Mommy Malone and Poppy Malone with grandkids. Carol is the short girl on the left with an arrow and Thomas is the short boy behind Poppy with an arrow. Gwin and Jean are Carol's upper left shown by arrows.

Willie Blanch Horton Malone and
Thomas Seabron Malone, circa 1957

Lorren Gwin Malone and Thomas Malone scuffling with an unknown friend in front of the Powell (Pal) Place, circa 1948-9

When Buntsy Was A Baby

Such a long time ago.
Before....
before she married and made me,
not so many years after her own mother had had her
not too many months after a wedding
of two young people setting out.
For her, as it was for her parents,
growing up happened quicker in those days.
Children came quicker and oftener.
So Buntsy didn't get to be a baby long.
No wonder it was the name she loved.
Little wonder in her last years that the old
woman always answered best to the old nickname,
smiling sweetly, readying herself to go,
'cause Mama was back home with Papa
waiting for Buntsy's return.

Now as I approach my own later years,
I'm feeling more and more like Buntsy,
remembering more clearly every day
those faces no longer seen.

Carol M. Siskovic
May 7, 2016
(My mother, Willie Blanch Horton Malone, Buntsy,
would have been 110 years old on May 4, 2016)

My “Precious”

A mere photograph.
Lost forever, I believed.
Only a dim memory.
Of myself and a dog named Scotty.
A pet I had held on to, I was told,
as I slowly learned to walk.
My first teacher.
One of my first loves.

A picture taken by an aunt,
at a time when few had cameras.
Photo of a toddler and her dog near a rosebush,
her hand grasping his back,
as both turned to look in unison,
questioning together,
“Who calls? What calls.”

And now, in a bottom dresser drawer
buried in a box of scattered items,
here it was, after so many years,
a return ticket to a feeling I had forgot,
a warm surge of comfort, safety.
And I just wanted to hold on.

Carol M. Siskovic

Elegiac Fever

Snowball, my Snowball puppy,
all white and fluffy, all mine,
wriggling in my little arms.
We stood at the front gate,
me still in my flowery pink pajamas,
watching the yellow school bus pull away,
windows full of laughing faces.
So enticing…then Snowball leaped,
yelping and circling into the grinding wheels.
Stop! Stop! The bus braked and a white flurry
darted backward in maddened white pain.
The back wheel, part of some fated team,
did its job and left behind a lifeless fluff,
soft hair tossing in the morning breeze
My four-year-old heart learned grief instantly,
and as I patted over and over
the unmoving sweetness, my mind understood,
"This is what **dead** is!"

Carol M. Siskovic

A Dog's Life

My Collie dog, Jenny, had two jobs,
one taught, assigned, expected.
The other adopted naturally out of love.
Each morning she was instructed,
"Jenny! Take the cows out"
And off she ran to bark those huge animals
all the way to the back pasture to graze.

She always returned in time to
sit erect at the side gate and watch me
board the school bus after giving her
a last goodby pat before parting.
Every afternoon when I returned,
nothing seemed to have changed.
There she sat wearing her typical smile,
a panting, patient, friendly acceptance
of "This is who I am, what I do."

Later in the day, she would leave me,
like clockwork, head for the back pasture.
Soon, I'd hear the lowing, complaining
cattle returning for the evening milking,
the night feeding, the settling in for all of us.
Mornings, nights, all my life,
I have carried in my mind's eye that devoted stance,
that look of inner pleasure at knowing and
doing the right thing because it is expected.
A life well-lived, a happy life, being faithful.

All other lessons I have learned lean
on that indelible one that Jenny taught.

Carol M. Siskovic

Cold Sauce

Every morning, every night,
I take the can of cat food from the fridge,
Pry off the red plastic lid and peer
Into the amber slime surrounding the mush.
Fumes of fish parts and meal rise
To mingle with the urgent meows.
I pour dry pellets into two bowls,
Then divide the wet food — two plops —
And cover each round hard bit
With fragrant meaty sauce.
They hate the dry food alone,
Leave it to the point of starvation,
But this concoction they devour,
Crunching through the bad hard kernels,
Licking at the cold sauce, and
I stir and think, and stir and think,
"This is their life, their joy."
I can almost hear myself meowing.

Carol M. Siskovic

Daily Lesson

Old, old cat
scruffy
near twenty now
waiting by the door
no longer allowed in
too untrustworthy
but still hungry
always ready to eat
still eager for strokes
leaning to the love
but sometimes the sudden bite
surprises both of us
a trigger that won't untrain
still playing the role assigned
comfortable enough
but wants in
waiting, just waiting
long naps, vigilant watching
staring at kitten years
more long naps
one day soon
something will have called
and something
will have answered
there will be no sign
just an empty space
and the silence of dignity
a door opened…then shut.

Carol M. Siskovic

2

I had three siblings. My older brother Lorren Gwin Malone, was almost 12 years older than I. My sister, Myra Jean Malone, was 10 years older. And my younger brother, Thomas Wade Malone, was not quite eight years older. I have no memory of spending much time with them as a kid growing up. Supposedly, my older brother Gwin carried me around when I was a baby. Everybody always joked when he got older that while he was tall and handsome, he sort of slanted his shoulders toward the right. He said the reason he walked like that with his left shoulder up in the air was because he always carried me on his left hip, and that affected his posture. I don't have any memory really of spending time with him until I was old enough to beg him to read the Sunday "funny papers" to me. By pointing to the words he read, he probably was my first teacher and those were my first reading lessons. All my life, anytime I ever looked in his eyes, I had that feeling that he was somebody who was very close to me. We'd look at each other, and I always felt very comfortable with him although I didn't remember or know why. But I knew it was there. When he joined the Army at age eighteen and went overseas, I really missed him. I remember that he sent me a pair of Japanese silk pajamas for Christmas which I would still have if they had not eventually burned in our house fire.

My sister, Jean, and I slept in the same bed together once I was old enough to sleep in a big bed. We shared a bed until she left when she was 18 and I was eight. She graduated from high school, got a job in Clarksdale and moved to a rooming house. A woman rented a room in her house to three girls. She provided them with breakfast and dinner, and they would take a sack lunch to work. Every Saturday, I would take her fresh washed and ironed clothes up the stairs to her room; then, together we'd take her dirty clothes down to the car to be put in the Monday wash. When she was nineteen, she married Paul

Broadway, the boy she had been dating. They gave no warning to the family of any wedding plans. After the Friday afternoon wedding, her best friend came to our house with her husband to tell us that they had stood with Jean and Paul as they got married at a preacher's house. My mother stood at the back steps wiping her hands on her apron, obviously so upset, but thanking them for telling her. I couldn't understand why we hadn't known or why my mother was so unhappy. I later learned that Jean was afraid our parents would not approve of the marriage so she gave them no say in the decision.

Rather than waiting to be drafted, my older brother, Gwin, joined the Army and served from the time he was 18 to 21, almost 22. He joined so that he could have some choice about what he did, and he was lucky enough to be taught photography and to be sent to Japan where, from an airplane, he helped photograph the bombed ruins of Hiroshima, Nagasaki, and other damaged areas. When he came back, he only stayed a short time before he left and moved to Memphis. He had started dating a high school girl, Wendy Whitworth, and had asked her to quit school, marry him, and move to Memphis where he was supposed to continue his study as a photographer. That soon became financially impossible, however, and he secured a lifetime job with Ford Motor Company. Then they proceeded to build their family of four children, Ronnie, Bethanne, Blake, and Scott. As the children grew older and married, they lived close by in the Memphis and north Mississippi area. Though Gwen and Wendy have passed, all the children still live there except for Bethanne who lives with her daughter and two grandchildren in Alabama. Gwin died in 2004, and Wendy died in 2011.

My brother, Thomas, graduated at 18, and went off to college. He had always loved sports and participated in football, basketball, and baseball so he wanted to become a coach. Coaches of small schools then taught every sport including football in the fall, basketball in winter, and baseball in the spring. He was the first person in our family to get a college education. He finished college at Delta State College in May, and immediately got a job at Crenshaw High School where he met his future wife, Lucy Goodwin. She was a senior at the time they met, and he knew her for one semester before he was drafted into the Army.

She said their dating was no problem then because girls often married at a young age and that it was often to older men. She said they just got their dating approved by the principal. Thomas had to leave in January for basic training in the Army, but he came back on leave in April to get married. Lucy finished high school and then joined him for his first assignment in Kentucky. When he finished his tour in the Army, they returned to Mississippi and continued to build their family of three children, Step, Chris, and Stacy. Thomas worked in several school systems as a coach, teacher, or principal until he retired, and they moved to a permanent home in Crenshaw, Mississippi, where she presently resides with her oldest son, Step. Thomas died in 2018.

So from age 10, I had no siblings at home except for brief visits. When I was very young, my cousin, Gerald Cooper, would come down from Memphis, Tennessee, and spend most of the summer with me as there was more for him to do on the farm than there was to do in the city during the summer. There were eight years between me and Thomas, my youngest sibling, but I had an almost brother in my cousin. He was just like a typical little brother, a big pest, but a lot of company. I really liked his being there because it wasn't as lonely for me. We would do all kinds of crazy things together, and I loved him like a brother.

One summer, we had gone out to the pasture, running along the fence, and then ducking in and out, antagonizing the bull. We were too scared to get very close, but we were having a lot of fun - so much fun running that we were covered with sweat. Gerald said, "I am going to go to the pool and wash my feet." We had been told to stay away from that pool. No one gave us a reason, we were just supposed to stay clear of it. The pool was not that big, but it did have a fence around it and a platform that made it easy to get up to and into. We climbed up onto the platform, sat down, and dipped our feet in the water. The next thing I knew, Gerald had slipped down into the pool and was up to his waist. Then he started jumping about and splashing, saying "This feels so good! Come on. It's fun." So finally, I joined him even though my Mother had always said, "Stay away from that pool." She had not explained why, but I thought it was because we couldn't swim. We had no problem wading around and splashing, and we must have done that for at least an hour.

Then we decided to get out and go home. As we were walking toward the barn on the dirt road, we noticed the mud on our legs was yellowish and stank terribly. We looked at each other and said, "What is this?" And even though we didn't quite understand, we somehow knew. That pool was off limits because that's where the toilet emptied out. We later learned it was called a cess pool.

We knew we'd better not let anyone know what happened so we went to the horse trough at the barn and tried to wash off. Mother came outside and spotted us. She went over to the peach tree and snapped a limb off and yelled, "You two get over here." Gerald started to run, but Mother caught his left hand with her left hand. They ran in circles as she spanked him. A dust cloud formed, and I stood frozen because I knew I would get a spanking as bad as his if I ran. She panted, "You two get back over to that trough. You wash yourselves. You wash your clothes, and don't you come in that house with a speck of mess on you." Nobody had to tell us ever again to stay away from the cess pool.

On another occasion, Gerald had ridden in the truck with Daddy to the "over back" to check on a tractor that had been having some problem. Daddy and the tractor driver decided to ride the tractor back to the barn to fix a part, so Daddy told Gerald to wait in the truck and they'd be back "tarekly." Of course, Gerald got bored and began fiddling around with the truck steering wheel, the starter button, whatever he could reach. We were all in the backyard as Daddy was finishing with the tractor when we looked down the gravel road and saw the strangest sight. Somebody was maneuvering Daddy's truck toward the corner turn, next to the dredgeditch, and it looked almost as if the truck was driving itself, and not very well! "Who's driving the truck?" everybody was asking. "Surely not Gerald!" "He can't reach the brake!" "And he can barely see over the steering wheel!" We watched as the truck somehow managed the sharp right turn and slowly weaved up the road toward us. As it came closer and closer, Daddy started running toward it. He caught up, then turned to run beside it, all the while shouting instructions to Gerald who was hanging on to the steering wheel with all his might. But he couldn't stop it, just barely steer it. Finally, as the truck got closer and closer to us, Daddy managed to jump on the running board and open the door and hit the brake, but not before we all scattered as the truck ran into our backyard fence, knocking it over.

"What were you doing? What were you thinking?" Everybody seemed to ask Gerald at once. "It just started up by itself!" Gerald answered with a sheepish grin. "All I could do was try to steer it!" Apparently, he had pushed the starter button, and the truck was getting just enough gas to edge forward without Gerald even touching the accelerator. Everybody agreed, finally, that he had done a pretty good job in his very first driving experience. Mother, of course, told Daddy it was pretty dumb to leave Gerald alone in a truck that could be cranked! Nobody else said anything to him, but everybody felt we'd been lucky that the worse thing was a toppled fence that could be fixed. Gerald just kept grinning sheepishly. Sometimes, I wonder if he ever remembers that first drive as he steers his side-by-side all over the North Mississippi farm he owns and stays active on, though he is now in his eighties.

That and many other experiences in the summers we spent together, made me feel like Gerald Cooper was more of a sibling to me than a real sibling might have been. As we grew older, we were lucky if we saw each other every few years at a family reunion, but early togetherness has always made me feel a special closeness to him. The last time I visited him after both our mates had died, he drove me all over his farm in that side-by-side, showing me his accomplishments. Just like old times!

At family gatherings, on both sides, I spent most of my free time with cousins. Early on, I became close to brothers Jackie Joe and Gary Ray Davis on the Malone side of the family, sons of my Aunt Trudy, my Dad's sister. I also played with Billy Joe Waldrop, Aunt Flossie' son, and Tommy Waldrop, Aunt Clara's son. My girl cousins included Eva Hardy and Peggy Hardy, daughters of Daddy's youngest sister, Aunt Marynell as well as Martha Jane, daughter of Daddy's only brother,

Uncle Jim Frank. That was seven cousins on the Malone side. On the Horton side, I was close to three girl cousins, Ann Horton, daughter of Uncle Bill Jack, and Virginia and Betty Horton, daughters of Uncle Roy Claude. These three girls and I met recently in Memphis to recall old times and early memories. So, in my youth, these ten cousins along with Gerald Cooper were my playmates. Together, we learned many life lessons. But as years went by, we saw less and less of each other.

Gerald always came in June and left in August. The rest of the year I was by myself nearly all the time. So I really don't have a lot of experience with siblings as pals. I remember my youth as being lonely, because I didn't even get to spend a lot of time with friends.

Even when I was in high school I didn't have many friends that lived close by. I had people that I knew at school, but we didn't spend much personal time together. When I went off to college, I joined a sorority, Beta Sigma Omicron, which no longer exists today since it merged with Zeta Tau Alpha. I got to know these girls and became such good close friends with all of them that many of us are still friends to this day. Amy Wilkinson Wittenberg lives in Memphis, Tennessee; Faith Craig West lives in New Albany, Mississippi; Betty Lou Tynes Adamson lives in Seattle, Washington; Lois Lawson Naul lives in Battle Creek, Michigan, and Jane Taylor lives in Tuscaloosa, Alabama. After all these years, more than 50, even living so far apart, we have remained friends, and those friendships are so dear to me. All these relationships helped me realize how important good friends can be in life. It made me want deep friendships in work, in marriage, and with my children and their spouses. Friends and Family! That's what counts in life.

Left to Right: Gwin, Jean,
Thomas, and
Carol Malone, circa 1949-50

Carol Malone Siskovic and
Gerald Cooper 2022

Childhood Memories Make Me Smile

Who knew the big pond in the back pasture was a cess pool?
Sure, we'd been told "Stay away from there!" but nobody bothered
explaining why, and we got hot chasing the bull.
Boy, was that mud brown and sticky, but the water cooled our prickly legs,
and such fun to splash in our crazy battle game.
Worth my mom's furious whirling of the limber peach tree switch,
and her making us wash ourselves and our clothes in the horse trough!

Who would ever think that cigarettes could make you hurl?
In the movies smoking looked so glamorous and all grown up.
The way you held it and drew in, then blew out with that look of
"God, I'm so great, I just love me."
We stole the stale pack of menthols someone had left behind,
and all afternoon hid ourselves, snickering behind the barn, then sick.
Ah, education, often painful and lasting - like a tattoo.

What would anyone expect from a horse named Dynamite?
Daddy bought her cheap: she was old, but gentle, perfect.
We rode her round the lot, all three aboard, taking turns being
middle man 'til we got brave enough to go it alone.
Such patience we found on her long, slow treks away from the barn,
mixture of wired and scared, 'cause we soon learned,
with her head turned toward home, she'd prove her name again.

Can driving a car be that different from driving a tractor?
My brother had plowed fields since he was eleven, kept straight rows,
clutching, shifting, steering like Ol' McDonald.
At fifteen he thought it time to get a driving license.
Dad agreed, said, "Git in the truck, son, give it a go, see how you do."
It cranked, it died, cranked, died, cranked, died, then he gave it the gas!
And steered it like a race car through the broad side of our storage shed.

Is staying quiet in church really necessary?
My friend and I sat up close in the second row and sang.
Lord, how we sang. and then the sermon started and continued.
And continued until we just had to whisper back and forth.
She said the funniest things, and our huddled heads shook
with youthful joking, unmoved by religion stuff.
From five rows back, aim as sure as David's.
Granny Cagle fired a songbook.

Direct hit! Salvation Day!

Carol M. Siskovic

The Universal Saga

Are my Live Oaks happy or hurting?
I watch the trimming team,
listen to their sawing, to the thumps
of falling cut limbs, now discarded
from the body that once held them.

A kind of death, or a means of renewal?
The tree trunk will grow anew,
now lightened and reaching at its tips.
The separated parts will be rendered
into chips that will find new purpose.

Will we, too, find another way to exist?
Will our disintegrating parts feed and persist?
The joy and support we have given remembered?
Will part of us provide, provide, through time —
a treasured piece of Life's eternal rhyme?

"Nothing remains the same," the saws sing.
Every lifeform grows, becomes, changes
until it joins a different part of a different heart.
Another limb falls. I think of loves departed.
And the passing years. So much started, restarted.

Carol M. Siskovic

Next To…

In my memory, she balances the wash
Her gray wrinkled hands shriveled
by the hot water from the black tub.
With tired fingertips she worships
the cleanliness she herself has created.
Sweaty, oily, dirty cloth transformed
into newness and sweetness.
Only the sun's crisp touch is needed now.
Then the pressure of her iron as she listens to the radio
Her loved ones will be covered by,
nestled by what she herself has done.
Nothing in her life is more satisfying or Godly.

Carol M. Siskovic

First Memory

3

One of the assignments that I always gave my students was to record the very first memory of their lives, so I often revisited my own. We can be surprised by what they are and how they make us feel. My first memory was of an experience in our sharecropper's house on the Johnson-Muse Road. That would have made me about four years old. I had the feeling that I was very small in this memory, and it begins with me lying on the kitchen floor. I am bored, so I am entertaining myself by rolling about. I know it is a brand new linoleum rug that my mother has just put down on the kitchen floor, and it is so smooth and clean feeling. There is a sink at a window where my mother and a woman I know are working and talking.

I can see their feet and their legs, but I'm rolling on the floor because I don't have anything to do or anything to play with. I am just rolling and looking, and rolling and looking. And as I roll to the edge of the linoleum rug, I start just sort of picking at the edge, and my mother starts telling me to stop it, a bit more harsh each time she spots me doing it. I know I might ruin the rug. And then I roll back, up to the edge of their feet, and I can see up their dresses. And that is a "no no," but so interesting to look way up! My mother snaps, "Carol, stop that. Get-away!"
I roll away to the edge where there is a table. My mother then sets a plate on the table, and it has a cake on it. I have the feeling that the cake is for me. As I roll back and forth, I look up, but I really can't see their faces in my memory. I do know that the woman with my mother is named Sarah.

I was told years later that Sarah spent a lot of time taking care of me, and that I cared a lot about her. I learned that she was Sarah Vanlandingham who had married a young man named Zeke

Vanlandingham, nephew to Big Mommy Malone, my dad's mother. I know that this was in the 1940s, and Zeke was away at war at that time, then came home later with differences that ended his marriage. I suppose that Sarah had walked over that day to talk to my mother and they were discussing very serious things as I kept rolling and rolling, and just wondering what to do with myself. I guess you could call my first memory a recollection of boredom. It may even be a birthday memory of April 29, 1943, if that cake was really for me.

Carol with a dolly

Carol Malone, age 3 with Scotty Dog

My Favorite Toys As A Child

Some childhoods have no toys or, like mine, a few.
What I remember most were some little cars and toy guns.
  A favorite play place for us was under the house,
  building roadways in the soft cool dirt.
    Or in the entire outdoors - riding our stick-horses
    into wild shootouts, firing bang-bangs
    at the "bad guys," knowing we were some of
    the good ones - heroes coming to the rescue.

Not that we had much choice as to where
we played, moved by that constant incentive:
  "You kids git out'a'doors rite now!"
  Besides, if we stayed in, we got put to work,
    and work hardly ever interested us.
    The outside world, though, held adventure.

Early lessons lurked in daily playtime dangers.
Be aware of what's around you.
  Fun fields held stickers and thorns.
  Never assume you'll be okay.
    Good hiding places also hide snakes, spiders.
    Around the next corner, who knows?

Watchfulness can sometimes be the best gift.
Uncertainty, they say, may be life's only certainty.
  Toys or no toys, though, games will be played.
  And almost anything becomes a toy if
    it draws a smile or provides a thrill or
    produces a companion also wanting to play.
Thinking on it now, who knows? My favorite childhood toys
  might have been an old coffee can and a whittled stick.

Carol M. Siskovic

Mother's Birthday Cakes

Mother always baked a cake
Your favorite if you had one
I don't remember presents
She got us what we needed
and said "That's your birthday"
sometimes weeks ahead, or after,
if we couldn't get to town
but the day was marked at the table
You could smell it early
sometimes at breakfast
She always did her cooking in early morning
While the frosting simmered
beneath her turning spoon
the layers would be set out to cool
She'd pour sugar water over each loaf
She liked to make round cakes
stacked four layers high with frosting between
Like an artist mason she'd smooth
and place and shape the light
delectable tower of airiness
into a declaration of you being special
Never any decorations or writing
Just the many-colored candles saved
from who knows how many cakes before
Exactly your number
to be wished on and blown heartily
toward the place where wishes go to hope
At that moment with the flames rousing,
forcing the wax downward like butter
all the light centered on you
You were the only one on this day -- your day
This day of separation
This day of setting out
And the cake said "I'm for you
I burn for you
Each year I burn more for you"
Such a lovely lovely light!

Carol M. Siskovic

Chicken, Cakes, and Flowers

4

Several times a year when I was growing up, Mother would order baby chicks by the box of 100, and the mailman would bring them and leave them at our mailbox. All the mailboxes for the people living on our place werc lined up on the side of the road leading into our farm. That was a good long walk from our house. It wasn't so bad if you drove it, but if you walked it, it would take 10 to 20 minutes to walk to and from the mailboxes. So when the chickens were due to arrive, Mother would send me over there to check and see if they had come. If they had arrived, I would see the box of chickens propped on top of the line of mailboxes. I didn't even have to go all the way to see them. So then I would run across the field rather than on the road, yelling my news, "They're here!"

Then Daddy would have to get his truck and go to the mailbox and put the box of chickens in there because it was too big for anyone to carry. I remember that they didn't come in the heat of summer. They always came when it was coolcr. The first thing Mother would do was to put them in the kitchen and check to see if they were okay. There would always be some that were smothered. She'd take out the ones that had not survived and dispose of those. I remember her having to put a light bulb over the box so that the little chicks would warm up. The ones that were not so healthy she would keep in the kitchen and nurse and feed them with an eyedropper to help them survive.

Those that were healthy, she would take and put in a pen out in the chicken yard that also had a light bulb and was nice and warm. It was just a wire cage inside the chicken house, and the little chickens would grow there. It would be my job sometimes to take food to them. I knew my mother loved those chickens as if they were her own children. But as they grew and got big enough to cook, she would have to go out to the yard and decide which chickens she would give up. She always cooked about 4 to 8 chickens on a Sunday. I realized later how difficult that must have been, a lot like picking among her own children to sacrifice for everybody to be able to eat.

I often watched her kill the chickens, and it was a quick death. She would grab the chicken and pet it and hold it and it would be clucking. Then she would hold the body of the chicken in her left arm. She would take her right hand and put it around the neck of the chicken, give it a final pet, then take that neck and sling it with one gigantic swing of her arm. That swift action killed the chicken immediately, and it never felt anything. Then she would put it on the block where she would take her axe and cut the head off the chicken. Then she'd throw it and all the other disposable parts into a can. Everything in the can was fed to the pigs later.

If you didn't kill a chicken right, it could get away from you. I've seen chickens that had their necks wrung, get away, and run all over a chicken yard. But *she* never did that. My husband always told a story about how as a boy he had rung a chicken's neck one time and it got away from him and ran into the pond. His grandmother, Baba, made him go into the pond and get wet to the waist up to bring her that chicken so she could finish it off and cook it.

After my mom killed a chicken, she worked quickly. It wasn't fast enough for her to pluck the feathers away, plus she didn't like to pluck them. When you plucked the feathers away, you had to have your water boiling to dip the chicken and then pluck those feathers out as fast as you could. That was a lot of hard work, and not too many people liked doing it. Instead, she would put the chicken down on a block, take her knife and cut the skin away. She knew exactly how to do it quickly and cleanly. The skin went in the bucket along with the head. She would open up the body of the chicken and take out all the entrails, vessels and everything uneatable. Then she would place the good remainder of the chicken into a dish pan and go to the next chicken. She would usually have 4 to 8 chickens ready to cut and cook when she got in the house. She would half each chicken and quickly cut the halves into four or five pieces, and fry them all up so fast that she was done before nine o'clock on a Sunday morning. Everybody always loved her fried chicken, and anytime we had any dinner or family reunion, everyone would say, "Give me Blanche's fried chicken. She makes the best fried chicken in the world!" But she also cooked a lot of other dishes that were equally desirable, like her dressing, her sweet potato casserole, and her pies and cakes. People loved her lemon and coconut pies and they loved her coconut cake, her chocolate cakes and her German chocolate cakes particularly. That was my favorite.

Mother and daddy never did do much for birthday presents. But they always celebrated the birthdays on the day of the birthday. Our gift was to choose the kind of cake that we wanted. I usually chose German Chocolate, and my brother Gwin always chose plain chocolate. Jean chose coconut cake, and Thomas liked pecan pies rather than a cake at all. But we would always get our choices. I don't even remember singing Happy Birthday. Maybe we did, but I have no memory of it. I do remember that the birthday person got to cut the cake or the pie or whatever and take as much as they could eat before others got any of it.

It took me years to even begin to understand how much my mother sacrificed to make all our meals special, especially on our birthdays. We may have taken her hard work for granted, but something of her caring character grew in each of her children so that, as adults, we too wanted to give of ourselves even in the smallest, daily, often unappreciated ways.

As I grew older, my life was comfortable, and I was grown before I really understood that it had taken my mother and father twenty years of marriage and share-cropping to save enough money to purchase their own place. They had to have an adequate down payment and then be able to make yearly payments on their loan. Such an agreement required that they produce profitable crops each year. In the deep south, that was often impossible. The saying was that "Three bad crops would ruin you."

I was 4 years old when we moved to the "Pal Place," and I was fourteen when we had to move away. At that time, they were unable to make their yearly payment, and Daddy had to take a job as a manager for another man's farm. They had arranged for my sister Jean and her husband Paul to move into the "Pal Place" house and let me live with them to finish my ninth grade year at Clarksdale High School. This all caught me by surprise. I was simply told in January that that was the plan. It didn't seem to affect me very much, and I liked living with my sister and being with my 2 year old nephew Terry every day after school. My parents moved into the manager's house on Blue Lake Plantation which was attached to a country store for the manager and his wife to run. My parents' plan was that they would work at Blue Lake until they could save enough to make their yearly payments and afford to move back and farm their own land. Meanwhile, they would rent out their farm land, and my sister would live in our house rent-free. My Dad would pick me up to spend each weekend with them, and I was expecting to be at Blue Lake with them all summer. Things, however, did not work out as planned. My parents had fully appreciated being able to own their own place. They'd worked consistently and diligently to purchase and then hang on to it, but life is unpredictable.

My mother had often said, "I've cleaned up enough old houses to last me a lifetime." And my dad had loved not having to move every few years. It was understood that Dad's job was taking care of the big crops and harvest. My mother's job was keeping a garden, raising animals for food, raising children, and making the house look as beautiful as she could. Both their jobs had required every hour of every day. But I will say that Daddy had more time off and Mother never seemed to have any. Each of them, however, did take a little time after lunch every day. Daddy would sit in a rocker after lunch and take a 20 minute nap, holding his newspaper, and Mother would listen to a soap opera on the radio. Then it was "back to work." With any extra time that Mother had, she was always trying to make things grow. In her chicken yard, in her garden, and in the front and side yards of the house. People said that her yard was the prettiest anywhere around. She had all kinds of blooming flowers. In the front of the "Pal" house, she'd placed a huge circular flower garden. Everyone around came to get roses on special days like Father's Day and Mother's Day when it was customary to wear a red rose for a living parent or a white one for a parent that had passed away. She'd taken great pride in being able to supply Cagle's Crossroads with all the roses that they would need.

Mother had always grown everything we ate, like cabbage, peas, beans, tomatoes, spinach, and corn. Also, Daddy grew whole fields of corn. Together, they'd planted 150 peach trees plus various apple trees, cherry trees and a few pecan trees. These would sometimes be used in making delicious treats, or sold to purchase other items that couldn't be grown. My brother Thomas and I spent a lot of time riding around the countryside in the jeep with bushels of fruit for sale, and we hardly ever came home with many left.

This was their life and mine for a good ten years. I remember them as steady, dependable years with my parents always hard at work, except for weekends when we went to town (Clarksdale) on Saturdays to shop and visit with everyone there. We often saw movies, either on Friday nights in the nearby town of Tutwiler or on Saturday afternoons in Clarksdale. I was always fascinated by the name of the little movie theater in Tutwiler and loved to say it as a kid. It was named after the four nearby small towns, Tutwiler, Rome, Vance, and Sumner. I loved saying we were going to the Tutrovansum! The last time I drove through Tutwiler, the only trace left of the Tutrovansum was the concrete slab it had been built upon. I remembered the time my cousin, Jackie Joe Davis, had jumped up and run up the steps onto the stage in front of the screen yelling, "I'll help you, Roy, I'll help you!" Roy Rogers probably never knew he had such support from his viewers.

We finished the weekend the same way every week as we never missed church on Sundays, morning and night, and often had dinner on the ground. Our other main entertainment was gathering at numerous family outings. Those early years for me proved busy and difficult in many ways but also full, fruitful, and hopeful. Then, with financial problems and the move, everything began to change.

TIME SAVER—T. S. Malone, poultryman of Minter City, Miss., checks an automatic waterer in his 10,000 capacity broiler house at his farm. Mr. Malone's watering system saves time and provides the broilers plenty of cool water.

Thomas Seabron Malone in the newspaper for their chickens.

A photo of Carol, age 6

Daddy is the man in back row with the hat.
This picture was taken in 1949 in front of Cagle's Crossing Church, located 3 miles south of Dublin , MS. The arrow is pointing to Mrs. Ola Mae Lesley. Thomas Malone is on her left.
Carol Malone is the taller girl in the front row.
Mother is behind him. Brother Bryant, our baptist preacher, is the man in front with a hat. Mrs. Bryant is beside him

Just Dig In

In my kitchen, I keep reminders.
On a shelf sits the sugar bowl that held
center place on the family table of my youth,
each person able to sweeten to taste.

On a hook hangs a huge iron skillet that slowly
perfected so much farm-raised beef, pork, chicken,
or multitudinous garden vegetables with cut field corn,
or anything edible that nature sent our way.

These kitchen necessities now serve as symbols:
representations of both Daddy (farmer, butcher, Provider-King)
and Mother (Comfort-Queen who kept us fed, full, satisfied).
Those necessary tasks, taken for granted, feed us still.

Whenever I touch an old familiar apron or prize spatula,
I hold not just memories, but values and sacrifice
that may be disappearing amidst our modern ease.
I remember… sigh. Then turn my thoughts toward
now, and tomorrow, which will forever entice.

Today, our meals, often "store-bought," "on-the-go,"
or "frozen" microwavable dishes, we devour as we
also consume some form of fascinating technology.
And sharing any family conversation as we "restore"
may now dwell in the imaginary Land of Nevermore.

Progress sets a different table in Time's kitchen.
Today's food chefs may "serve" as heater/consumers.
Sometimes, we also warm up a dish of memory.
Mostly, we keep memories on ice in case of
a sudden unexplained hunger.

Carol M. Siskovic

Awakening

I think of a tree full of brown sparrows.
Sparrows my farm parents resented.
Their constant pecking at ripening fruit,
gardens, and chicken feed just a nuisance.
I recall how no one ever minded
when my brother and his friends
practiced their shooting on the birds,
leaving dead carcasses as surprises
for the cats to find and drag away.
Permanently impressed on my mind
as with a branding iron, stays
a single moment of being allowed a turn,
of lifting the heavy rifle toward open sky,
asking, "What should I shoot at?"
The reply: "Anything!" and I pull.
Imagine our open mouths, then loud cries,
when one fleeing bird happens to occupy
at just the right millisecond
the same space as my carelessly sent bullet.
The boys exclaim, "Way to go!"
My daddy grins.
What a shot! Another scavenger gone.
No loss, just gain.
No grief, no reproval.
My bare feet wriggle in the loose, dry yard dirt,
digging in, latching on.
I had grown up midst the commonalities of
choosing chickens for Sunday dinner,
waking early for busy hog-killing days,
"taking care" of egg-eating dogs, or wild creatures.
But now… the rifle retrieved, my hands hang empty
… and I am disarmed.

Carol M. Siskovic

A Pot in the Attic
(Dedicated to the Phil Whittenberg family, & their pot)

It's in my head, I think of it every so often.
Up there, gathering dust, coated in its past.
Big, round, dented copper container.
I try to picture the far-back grandfather
forming the wrought iron rim and handle
to finish off this perfect piece of cookery.
I think of how many fruit trees they planted,
how many sweet harvests they gathered.
The mountains of homegrown apples bubbling
into dippers and dippers of delicious applesauce
served to how many eager open family mouths.
I think of its own long journey from Virginia,
by wagon maybe, across the Mississippi,
all the long way to Turkey Creek, Missouri.
Then years later, discovered hanging unused
on a hook in the back of an old chicken house,
Gramma no longer needing to stand outside
tending a fire, stirring and chopping in apples.
It took a grandson to see value and history,
to hear the echoes, rescue ancestral handiwork,
to save it, move it with him to Oklahoma, then
Mississippi, Tennessee, house to house to house
through years of children and grandchildren.
Maybe some of them crawled inside to hide,
maybe toys rattled around, along its edges.
Maybe it stored blankets or held dirty clothes.
Who knows the uses and the ways it served
before it rose, hidden away at its present height.
Long hours, it may dream of a loftier future,
housed in prominence at some grand museum
or used at special times to teach ancient ways.
It may picture its maker's yet unborn descendants
climbing up for an attic adventure, spying a glint
beneath the dust, wiping a swath, rediscovering
the tarnished copper beauty of a trusted old friend.
Dare hope their fingers will feel electric messages
passed hand to hand to hand -- their heritage.

Carol M. Siskovic (June 8, 2016)

Every December I Remember…

My father driving our old black Chevrolet,
My mother on the benchseat beside him.
I can only see their shadowed backs
And the occasional flash of passing lights.
They're talking in murmurs, I try to listen
But my eyes and head are so heavy.
It's Christmas Eve and we're headed home
After the picture show at the Tutrovansum Movie.
I feel tingly with the possibility
That Santa is at our house right now
Chuckling, tiptoeing, nibbling cookies,
Placing his magic near my penciled note.

Carol M. Siskovic

Grandparents

5

I grew up with two sets of grandparents. My mother's parents were Emma Belle Ramay Horton, and Will Horton. We called them Mama Horton and Poppa Horton. They were both a very quiet sort of people. They didn't talk a lot even though they had nine children. Maybe because of that! There are only a few times in my life I remember them actually talking to me. There's a story about when I got a doll for Christmas when I was about three to five years old. We went to their house for a Christmas visit, and my grandfather was sitting on a stool by the fireplace when we walked in as I carried my new doll, an armful for me. I have a memory of seeing him there without a smile on his face. And he says, "Bring me your baby. Let me see your baby." I screamed, "No!" I remember hugging that doll that I didn't yet really care a lot about. But I wasn't going to take it over to him because I really didn't know who he was. I remember clearly that my dad swatted my rear end and was going to make me show him until Poppa insisted that it was okay. That's a very brief memory, but it shows I did not feel close to them. I did not really learn a lot about them until much later in life, but I found they had very interesting lives.

Emma Belle Ramay Horton was the child of Miles Ramay who had fought in the Civil War, the War Between the States. As Emma's children grew up, they became very curious about their grandfather's family. My Aunt May, Mother's older sister, began trying to find out about Miles Ramay's family because he had lost all contact with them. He didn't know if they were living or dead, and he was truly afraid to learn how they had all fared. So she wrote a letter addressing it to General Post Office, Ramay Family, Des Moines, Iowa, saying that Miles Ramay had come from Des Moines, Iowa, had grown up there, then had moved to Missouri where he had joined the Confederate Army with his co-workers at the outbreak of the Civil War. The letter actually got to them.

Aunt May had written, "We may have cousins there as our grandfather is Miles Ramay. He grew up in the Ramay family, but he chose to fight on the side of the South." She explained how toward the end of the war he was wounded and left at a farm house in North Mississippi. After he recovered and the war ended, he felt too embarrassed to try to go back to see if any of his family was still there. He thought it was possible that he might've killed some of his own brothers in the war. He couldn't face that possibility. She explained, "He is older now, and we would like to know something about his family. Is there anyone left in Des Moines, Iowa, who is the family of Miles Ramay?" Miles Ramay's mother was still alive and wrote back.

She replied that the family would like to see him again before she died. She said his father had died the previous year. They started planning to travel south, and it wasn't long until the mother and some of his siblings made a train trip down to Memphis, Tennessee. In Memphis, they rented a horse and wagon, and they drove the distance from Memphis down to Coldwater, Mississippi, then on to LoveJoy, Mississippi. They reconnected with Miles there, so he got to see his mother and reconnect with family before she and he died. When she left, she said she was going to send them some of the things for his inheritance, and when they got back home, she shipped him an organ and a handmade wooden chest. She wanted her granddaughters to learn to play the organ, and the chest had been handmade by his father for the storage of the new baby belongings when Miles was born. In that chest was also a walking cane that his father had whittled and used toward the end of his life. The chest and cane were passed on to my son, Joel Elias Siskovic, II, "Lee," who happened to have the same color red hair as Miles Ramay. My Aunt Mae told me this story when Lee was about a year old. He was young, but she looked at him and said he had the exact same color hair as her grandpa had up till the day he died. I said, "But Lee's hair is blonde in the back," and she looked and replied, "Grandpa had a blonde streak in the back of his hair just like that!" So she insisted we take the chest and the cane that very day, that they be passed on to Lee from his great great grandfather, Miles Ramay, whose grave can be viewed with other family graves in the LoveJoy Church graveyard. I don't know what happened to the organ, but no one was available to teach my mother or her sisters how to play. She had high hopes that my piano lessons and the lovely carved rosewood piano she managed to buy would prove fruitful, but my piano teacher quit teaching, I didn't learn much on my own, and the lovely piano later burned with the house. She must be smiling somewhere today as her great grandsons, Shane and Miles, play beautifully for their own pleasure and for anyone who will listen.

Emma Belle Ramay Horton and Will Horton were very quiet people and didn't have a lot of stories to tell. I do remember one final visit with my grandfather. On that visit I got to see him not too long before he got sick and died. The rest of the family had gone out to the car, and I had gone to the bathroom and as I was coming out, I said, "Bye Poppa, I'm leaving." He stopped me and said, "Sit down, I want to talk to you." Then he started telling me the story of when he asked Mama Horton to marry him. I talked to my cousins recently, and none of them had ever heard this story. So far as I know, it was never told to anybody except me. He said, "I had been seeing your grandma, your Mama Horton, and I decided I wanted to marry her. So we had a horse, a white horse. We didn't have a saddle. So I put a halter on that horse, and I rode over to her house bareback. I rode as fast as I could and when I got there, she was out in the yard feeding the chickens. I rode up on the horse, and she looked up at me and smiled. I jumped off the horse, and I went over to her and I took her hand." He said he asked her, "Emma, will you marry me?" And she nodded her head and quietly said, "Uh-huh." Then he simply stated, "…and so we got married." I thought that was the funniest proposal I had ever heard. I told him goodbye, and that was the last time I ever saw Poppa Horton. For most of his life, he was not very talkative, but for some reason he chose to tell me that story the last time I saw him.

Funny that I only have two strong memories of Papa Horton, that last one and the uneasy first one, that Christmas memory. So I am very happy to retain such a warm final memory of him. Unfortunately, I have only one firm memory of Mama Horton, of her in the kitchen cooking and mumbling stories to me that I really couldn't hear very well. I was embarrassed to let her know my problem, and so I mainly nodded and muttered brief one-word responses.

My dad's mother and father, Willie Malone and Elizabeth Jane Vanlandingham Malone, were equally untalkative most of the time. Their friends called them Willie and Lizzie, but the grandkids called them "Big Mommy" and "Poppy" Malone. They had seven children and many grandkids so they only "babysat" me a few times even though we lived close by. I think both sets of grandparents did not pay much attention to all of their grandkids because they had so many of them. And it was a different time. I wouldn't say they didn't love us. It's just that they had so many grandchildren to get to know. Plus, I was the kind of child who was shy and not very outgoing. So I didn't get to know them as well as many of my cousins did.

Poppy Malone died when I was about six years old, and the thing I connect with his death is that while he was in the Clarksdale hospital, the family stayed at a hotel called the Alcazar Hotel. We went there and all stayed in one room waiting for news of his outcome as he was being treated in the hospital. At that time, not many visitors could stay at the hospital for long. To entertain ourselves, all the younger grandkids spent their time riding up and down in an elevator because none of us had ridden in an elevator very much. We had the time of our lives just going up and down and up and down all day long in the elevator.

When we got the word that he had passed, we left the hotel to prepare for his funeral. I don't remember anything about the funeral or anything much about him, but I do remember riding that elevator at the Alcazar Hotel. Later, they sold Mommie Malone's house and any property they may have had, and it was decided that she would spend about six weeks with every child and go from child to child, staying in their different homes. So she would come to us about twice a year. During those visits I did get to know her pretty well.

Big Mommie Malone told me a lot of stories because she could concentrate on me alone by the time she stayed with us. My two older brothers and my sister were grown, and they were not around very much or had already left the house. One day my teacher assigned us to ask our parents or grandparents about their life and to write up one of the stories to read to the class the next day. Big Mommie told me two stories.

The first was how some of Poppy's friends played a prank on him when he started to court her. Before they got back into his wagon after going to a church party, some of his mates shoveled manure onto the floorboards under the bench seat where it wouldn't be seen. When they got in the wagon, they couldn't understand why it stank so bad! It took a while for them to figure it out, and longer to clean it out for the ride home.

On another date, they were supposed to go to a party. It was fashionable for the girls at that time to wear bangs, but my grandmother's daddy would not let his girls cut their hair. Somebody gave her the idea that if she put lye soap in her hair, it would stiffen the hair. Then she could pin it in a roll and make it look like bangs. She did that, and her hair looked so nice. He picked her up in his horse and wagon, and they went to the party, but on the way back it started raining and the lye began to drip down on her face and into her eyes. She started crying, and she couldn't help it or stop crying because of her burning eyes. He kept asking, "What's the matter? What's the matter?" but she was too embarrassed and couldn't explain to him what she had done. When they got to her house, she muttered "I gotta go" and ran in the house. He thought that she was mad at him and was crying because he had brought her home in the rain with no cover. I didn't ask how long it took her to explain how she was at fault. I wrote those stories, and they proved favorites when I read them to the class. I think that is my first memory of being able to entertain with my writing.

Another story that sticks in my mind took place toward the end of her life when Mommy was about 94 or 95. One of my aunts had built a house for Big Mommie behind their house that had room for a full time nurse to stay there with her. So, at the end of her life, that was where she lived. My mother and dad would go and see her there every Sunday afternoon after church. I no longer lived at home but was living in Dallas at that time. The story was that my dad went to tell her goodbye as she was lying in her bed. He would usually say, "We're gonna go, Momma, bye." And she would say, "Bye, see you next week." But on this particular Sunday afternoon, she took his hand when he came to say goodbye. She looked at him and even though she was nearly blind, she looked him right in the eyes. And she said, "Bye, Son, bye." He went out to the car and they talked for a little bit, but before he could get in the car to leave, the nurse came out and said, "Your mom just died." He said that was very meaningful to him, that she looked at him, her oldest son, and, for the first time in many years, called him "Son" right before she died.

Mommie Malone and her son Thomas
Seabron Malone

Sarah Frances Morgan Ramay,
Mother's Aunt Sarah.
Mother wanted to name her last child Sarah Carol but settled for Frances Carol. Mother lived with Aunt Sarah and Uncle Johnny for a year in Clarksdale, MS. Uncle Johnny was the Ramay uncle who gave all the nicknames to everyone in the family.

Married: February
William Henry Horton
Emma Bell Ramay Horton

This is a house with rooms for rent in Calhoun City, Mississippi, where Lizzie and Willie Malone lived for a while with their family. Thomas Seabron Malone (called Seab) is in the front right wearing a cap and a light shirt. They probably lived there while they were waiting to find a place to sharecrop. Big Mommy, Seab's mother, Elizabeth Jane Malone, is standing in the middle back row (pregnant at the time?) next to the man holding a child, possibly Willie Malone(?). Seab"s older sister, Curtis (Curt) may be standing behind Seab to his right side. There may be other relatives in the picture, but none that have been identified.
Circa 1912 - 1915.

Holiday Away

It was like feeding a fragile sparrow.
Her little mouth opened and shut,
with its dryness echoing in my ears,
blindly sipping the orange juice, sucking
the smooth cool ice cream, her second favorite
all her life, after ripe red watermelon.
Accepting eyelids too heavy to keep open,
breathing soft and fluttery, she allowed me
to baby her, even loved my "mothering
of the mother," my stroking and tucking,
though she only murmured in dreamlike memory.
Her last words as I left: "I have to put up
the Christmas tree, find the lights."
In the morning hours she flew softly away
to spend her holiday without us,
her sweet song lingering through the years.

Carol M. Siskovic

Heading for a Hundred
(Destination: Neverland)

Because my life proves so complete
I dream and long for more.
This capsule that I move within
Has traveled miles galore.

Together - we have flown through time
And known the world's delights.
With troubles, too, though really few,
And persevered the fight.

I'm aged and worn, not nearly done,
And never bored or lax.
Both heart and soul reach forward still,
Life spirit barely taxed.

Low setting sun - not far away-
Vast fertile fields in sight.
Recess and joyful times can tempt
A change in speed of flight.

Both passenger and pilot - ME -
We like to think, with plan,
Sweep forward undenied and keen
To fly and never land.

But truth be told, a hundred years,
Our goal, would still fall short.
No vessel or no place exists
We'd want as final port.

Carol M. Siskovic

6

Since I grew up in the South, you would think I would have been very conscious of race relations. But I simply accepted things as they were and did not consider the major differences. I knew there were differences, of course, and that they often prevented different sides from blending. For example, Catholics and Protestants never worshipped together. Chinese stayed with Chinese people. Black people stayed around other black people. We shopped at Chinese groceries, black people did most of the field work, and Jews never worshiped with Christians. Those were commonly accepted behaviors. The one difference that was clearest to me, however, was financial. Rich people didn't associate with poor people. Poor people were considered "less than" by the rich. One of the reasons I eventually decided that I wanted to change schools and go to the school in town was because I thought I would get a better education and a better chance by going to school with people who were more "well-off."

I wrote a prize-winning poem about one of the first arguments that I ever heard between a white person and a black person. They were my dad and a black man who had owed him money for quite a long time. The altercation occurred in a rough building on our farm called the "shop" where my dad was working with his forge. I was playing on the dirt floor when the man came in to talk to my dad. I became aware that Daddy was very upset because he was supposed to be paid for something, and the man was unable to pay. That's when I noticed that the man's shoes had holes and his little toes were sticking out as he had no socks on. He also wore denim overalls with no shirt and only one strap was holding them up. As I watched, he took some change out of his pocket, held it out in his hand and said, "Dis is all I got. You can take dis." My dad said, "Put your money away. That's not nearly enough!" Then the man looked at me and said, "Here, little missy, you take dis." I reached for the money, but my dad yelled, "Carol, don't you take that money. Throw it down!" I let the money fall into the dirt but immediately stooped down to get it. I still visualize those coins lying in the dirt with my dad yelling, "Don't you touch'em!" And the black man stomping away. I didn't understand exactly what had happened or why. But I knew that it was a problem that couldn't be solved.

My memories of the Pal Place started when I was almost five years old. We moved there in January of 1944, and I turned five on April 29. My first and only memory of the move itself was of the night before we moved. I was kneeling before a fireplace, holding my hands up to the fire to warm them. Behind me, sitting on what must have been a bed or couch, were my Dad and two brothers. I suddenly realized Daddy was telling them what to do as we were moving the next day, and I was chilled at the thought. I can still hear myself asking, "Daddy, Daddy? Are we moving?" He gave some kind of abrupt positive answer, but I just remember that sudden flooding of extreme fear that filled me as I gazed into the blazing fire.

I have no other memories until we had moved to the Pal Place and my sister Jean and I got our own bedroom and were sleeping together. I don't have a definite memory of whether we shared a bed before that, but I have warm memories of sleeping in "our" bed that now is in Jean's house in Belzoni, Mississippi, where it has been since 1985. I slept with her in "our bed" from the time we moved to the Pal Place until she graduated high school at age 18 and moved into Clarksdale. Then I slept in it alone until the end of my ninth grade when the bed was moved to Blue Lake, then Minter City, Mississippi, where it was used by my parents. Then, after Daddy"s death in 1968, it was "Mother's bed" in two different homes in Memphis, Tennessee, and also when she moved in with my sister in 1985. It stayed with my mother through all her moves until it finally came with her to Belzoni, Mississippi, where it now remains. I still think of it as "my bed," and I sleep in it every time I visit, always remembering all that I have experienced with that bed, sleeping with my sister, my cousins and a few friends, then later my Mother, my daughters, and my husband. Not to mention the numerous times through the years that I lounged, bounced, or just sat and talked with that bed as my support.

I recall that as a child I never wanted to go to bed without my sister. Once when she wanted to go on a date with her friends to the movies, I cried and begged her to take me too. Then she thought and said, "What if I give you a nickel to let me go without you?" I thought how I could go to the store and buy a popsicle or a candy bar. Then I said, "How about two nickels?" She laughed but agreed. So I learned to go to sleep alone. But the bed itself has always been a comfort, and I hope at some time to reclaim it and sleep in it again. If not, I can always return to it in my memories and dreams.

After a series of horrible occurrences in 1954, there was no returning to our place at Cagle's Crossroads so Daddy sold our land, and I started my tenth grade year at West Tallahatchie High School in Webb, Mississippi. That turned out to be a good thing for me as I made new friends and experienced a more rewarding range of activities in both school and community. Looking back, I realize that with the terrible experiences, I began opening up more and seeking to broaden myself and my life, to find meaning and inner purpose.

In West Tallahatchie High School, I was elected as a class officer every year, and I took journalism and became involved in many school activities. A fellow classmate, Emma Flautt and I, as school paper and yearbook co-editors, were allowed a lot of freedom in covering stories for West Tallahassee High School. A really memorable experience was during the widely publicized trial of the men who killed the young Emmett Till from Chicago. The trial took place in Sumner, Mississippi, only a short distance from our school, so we were able to drive to observe the trial whenever we were free. I often drove our family car to school so we had the means to check out the trial a few times. We both had classes that we could be excused from during that trial so we were able to attend.

It was interesting to me because I had a cousin who, years before, had married early at the age of 18. When he was 19, he and a bunch of boys were in a truck wreck, and he had been one the several boys who were killed. His wife was young, still 18 or 19, and she remarried within a year or so. The person that she remarried was a man whose brother supposedly helped kill Emmett Till. So the trial was a little bit more personally interesting to me. Most of the people understood that those men really did kill Emmett Till because they thought he had not shown the proper respect for a white woman. Even though she was dressed in short shorts and a halter, they thought he didn't have any right to be whistling at her and making insinuating statements. Those men went to his grandparents' house that night and pulled him out to teach him a lesson. For whatever reason, he was killed, thrown in the Tallahatchie river, and later discovered. It was known that those man had gone to his house and so they were brought to trial. I don't remember all the facts about the trial, but I do know that they got off. I'm not sure exactly how that was settled, but the trial was a very memorable high school experience for me. That and many other high school experiences helped me develop a real interest in writing and journalism and all the aspects of literary expression, which led me to desire a college education and a degree in English and journalism. I finally settled on Millsaps College and a major in English for the purpose of teaching. Through the years, my interest in all forms of written expression has steadily deepened.

Courtroom scene during the Till murder trial
https://famous-trials.com/emmetttill/1755-home

Small Change

"Don't touch that money, Baby!
Leave it there! It can rot for all I care!"

I was already on my bare knees
in the cold cool dirt of the shop floor.
The heat from the Smithy and the still
summer day intertwined above me,
around the flaming faces of two big men
wearing farm clothes, damp and dusty.
The giant nearest me was my Daddy
dressed in khakis, cuffs frayed from always
slipping down to his heels as his trousers
lost the hitching battle with his Daddy belly.
He'd rolled his shirt sleeves high over his elbows.
His forearms holding the billows-handle looked hard,
like his jaw. Sweat poured down this face I thought I knew.
His mouth pressed tight, turning the scar on
his upper lip into a white streak of lightning.
He'd ripped his lip as a young boy flying forward over
a mule's head in a forbidden downhill race after school.
"Served him right," Big Mommie always said,
in a kind of boast, half proud, half righteous.
Now his soft hazel eyes glared at the black figure standing there.

Crouched between them, I looked from one to the other.
Bluejean overalls hung loosely on the other, strap dangling.
He wore no shirt. I wondered about the underwear.
I suspected there wasn't any. Just the britches,
hanging by the one strap, and old high-tops with no laces,
walked sideways so there were only half heels.
I could see one brown toe peering through a hole.
I couldn't move my eyes from that toe or get up,
but I didn't dare reach for the dull pennies he'd
thrown onto the ground at my father's feet.

Funny, I knew his name was Penny, too.

He lived in a sharecropper's house on my Daddy's place.
....Penny throwing away pennies....
There must have been ten or more of them.
Enough for a popsicle or a Co'Cola.
My fingers wanted them, but my ears burned
from the gunshot words exploding in the air above.
"No count.... Shiftless."
"Boss Man. White Gods."
"Don't pay your debts! Keep your word!"
"Can't keep me here. Hold me down."
"Sheriff after you. Haul your...."
"Take all I got. Squeeze me dry."
"You said...." "You lied...." "Might as well be dead."
"Take off then." "Go, you!" "Ain't never had no chance!
"Ain't never tried." "So...." "So...."

I couldn't breathe right, and I didn't know why I was crying.
With my finger, I started making overlapping circles in the gray silt.
Tears made little mud specks as they fell into the rings.
My hand abruptly scooped the nearest pennies, three or four,
and I stood stiffly, a palm full of dust and coins stretched
between the two of the men, like an offering.
"Give 'em to him!" my Daddy ordered.
"No, little missy, you keep 'em," Penny said.
"Throw'em down!" Daddy bit the words.
And suddenly, what I held was filth.
I turned my hand and watched them fall, then...
wiped the dirt against my thigh, afraid to look up.

I cannot remember any more. I know Penny left.
And years later, the shop burned and
someone sowed the whole place in beans.
I don't suppose anyone ever picked up those images of Lincoln.
They may be plowed under, deep in the southern dirt
that now covers both those men.

Carol M. Siskovic

Long and Hard

We weep at stories of struggle,
hurt for Eve and Adam outside the garden,
cry for little Ruby Bridges praying her way
to an empty school where she should have
been joined in learning with a hundred open hearts.
The loneliness, the hardness, squeezes us
to look across the fence to other yards, other roads.
And sometimes,
we do not wipe the tears away.
Sometimes, we wear the tears
and walk out to a new road,
or open our gate and invite in
all travelers on that long personal
trip toward self-understanding.

Carol M. Siskovic, 1996

Learning About Loss

7

Nothing distresses a child more than the loss of a favorite toy or trinket and how much more, the losing of something of true value. One of the hardest things to learn to live with is loss, and some begin to learn that very early on. When I was growing up, I had one really good friend. We saw each other every Sunday, and quite often we would go home with each other for the Sunday afternoon and stay all afternoon playing together. Her name was Murlyn Spurry, and she lived with her parents, Murl and Mary Spurry and her grandmother, Granny Cagle. She was a couple of years older than I was, so I remember that I was happy that she was already in school when I started to school. Because she was in a different grade, however, I didn't see her very much and then soon after that, she changed to Clarksdale Schools, so the only time I ever really got to see her was on Sunday at church and Sunday afternoon. I have many memories of all that we did together on those days.

She was such a daring person. One of the funniest memories happened at church. We were seated about three rows back from the front, and we had started giggling and whispering to each other while the preacher was preaching. Unfortunately, this distressed Granny Cagle to an extreme, and all of a sudden, a songbook came hurling through the air and hit us both square on the back of our heads. It made such a sound! We both gasped, and the whole church stopped dead. The preacher paused his preaching. You could hear those quiet little snickers when people realized that Granny had just taught us one of the best lessons that we would ever learn. Needless to say, Murlyn and I never again misbehaved in church. There's no greater teacher than a song book hurling through the air at you.

On Sunday afternoons we would go home with each other, and we would wander the neighborhood without any guidance at all. Murlyn was pretty good at getting me into some mischief. I remember that close to our mailboxes was a kind of a dredgeditch pond that had never looked inviting to me. It was covered with green moss and floating trash, but that didn't stop Murlyn. She insisted we take off our sandals and go wading. I have a vivid memory of overcoming my fear and splashing with her through green slime and slush for at least an hour. That helped me overcome my natural repulsion and fears of many natural areas around the farm and countryside.

One day, I got the news that Murlin was sick, was having to stay out of school, and had been out for maybe a few weeks. I had not seen her for a long while so Mother decided that we would go and visit with her. When we got to her house, Mrs. Spurry and Mother put me in a chair right beside Murlyn's bed which had been placed in the front room. They went to a table across from us to talk together, and I looked at Murlyn and she looked at me. I could tell immediately that she was so sick and was not herself at all. I tried so desperately to find something interesting to talk about, a good question to ask, but nothing would spur any conversation from her. She just looked at me in such a sad, sad way. It was almost as if we had already said goodbye, and she was about to leave. That was the feeling I had. I couldn't say anything. I couldn't do anything. I could barely stand to look at her.

She closed her eyes, and I just sat there and watched. I desperately looked over at my mother, and she looked at me and realized that I had to leave. So she whispered something to Mrs. Spurry and said aloud, "Well, we need to be going now. Carol, come on. Let's go." I can't even remember how we got there or left. My mother didn't drive very much, so I don't know if she drove us there or if my Dad was waiting outside for us. All I remember is my last look at Murlyn. I looked at her, and I said "Murlyn…bye" and she didn't respond. She just blinked her eyes. She didn't have the strength to say goodbye.

It wasn't long after, on a Saturday morning, that my dad came into the kitchen and said, "Bad news." I was in the next room, and I heard him and I looked up and saw his face. He said, "Murlyn's dead."

It hit me so hard. It still does today. Her life ended so quickly at twelve or thirteen years old. She had so much that she might have done. They thought it might have been Rheumatic Fever or a kind of cancer. In those days, nobody knew for sure. She had gone to a famous hospital in Memphis, but they said they had done all that could be done. I never forgot the lesson that I learned that day: Life is fleeting. We never know how long we have and must make the most of every minute.

Many years later at my mother's funeral, I was greeting people and Mrs. Spurry appeared. She hugged me, and I remembered Murlyn's funeral. The thing I remembered most about the funeral itself was that a girl our age sang "When They Ring Those Golden Bells For You and Me" and how afterwards, I sat alone in our car waiting for Mother and Daddy to come, and as we slowly drove in the funeral procession, I sang those words over and over in my head. It was perfect for her funeral. Even now, after all these years, whenever I have a chance to visit Oakhurst Cemetery in Clarksdale, Mississippi, I visit Murlyn's grave…and remember.

Hymnal like the one Granny Cagle threw.

How to Travel Lightly

Carry with you
  some small clue
    of happiness.
Wear the signs
  like green vines
    of yes, yes, yes.
Greet all you meet
  on bus or street,
    with a mental kiss!

Carol M. Siskovic

"Getcha Ready"

What a lovely day to be going!
With autumn in the air!
The grass has slowed and won't need mowing.
The harvest is in; you haven't a care.

Forget the clothes out on the line drying,
Don't worry on chores still undone.
Just pull on your "Sunday-go-to meeting."
Become one with the earth and the sun.

The planting is over, the tending complete;
The working and sweating are past.
The hard bitter winter, the wearing summer heat
Never brought pain that could last.

You battled and bickered and bargained,
Spat in the face of the wind.
You cried and you laughed and held to the end.
For you knew when to bow, when to bend.

The garden you carefully nurtured
Bursts with blossoms galore
And as each new cycle is ended
Springs back more full than before.

So glory in the flowers, scoop up the harvest.
Flow with the breeze that is blowing.
Smile, lean back, and let you be blessed.
It's a lovely day to be going!

Carol Malone Siskovic

(The title was my Daddy's oft-spoken entreaty
every time we were about to go somewhere)

8

When I was growing up, the only book in our house was the Bible, and the only other reading materials were the Farm Home Journal and the daily newspaper. On Sundays, my brother Gwin would always read to me what we called the "funny papers" from the Sunday newspaper, the Memphis Commercial Appeal. He would point to each frame and each word as he read. I did start reading the Bible at around 11 years old and by 11 or 12, Granny Cagle, our community and church matriarch as well as my best friend Murlyn Spurry's grandmother, realized that I was becoming a reader. She decided to give me a children's book of nursery rhymes as I seemed unfamiliar with them. When I began to read them, I realized that I had never been taught any of those nursery rhymes at all. Nobody had ever read them to me (or to my parents, I presume), and I had never seen them written down though they were all the typical rhymes like "Jack and Jill" and "Little Miss Muffet." Almost a teenager, I read them for the first time and really appreciated the gift. Years later as an adult living in England, I found it very interesting to visit areas where many such rhymes originated, like Banbury Cross for instance.

The very first book that I remember reading and actually enjoying ended up being my favorite book that I have ever read. My eighth grade English teacher, who was really a very strict, no nonsense teacher typical of the times, said, "All of you have to do a book report this six weeks, and you need to go to the library and choose a book. I will approve it, and you can read it, and then you will write a book report on it and turn it in at the end of the six weeks." So that afternoon, after school, I went to the school library, which was scary in itself.

The library was not very welcoming, nor the librarians, but I went in and was standing there kind of looking side to side, trying to decide which area to go into. The librarian saw me and she said, “What do you need!” just like that. I muttered, “Ms. Persons told me to come check out a book for a book report.” She crooked her index finger and said, “Come with me.” So I followed her over to a section. I didn't even get to choose the book. She ran her finger along the shelf, and she was looking, looking; I had no idea about any of them. Then she pulled out a book, gave it to me, and said, “Read this one.” I said, “What is it, Jane ….” And she said “Eyre, Jane Eyre, like air, but it's spelled E-Y-R-E. Just say it like A-I-R.” And I said, “Jane Eyre.” She stated firmly, “Good. I'll go check it out for you.”

I left; it was a Friday afternoon so I got on the bus carrying my big book with lots of words. I just didn't know how in the world I would ever get it done in six weeks. I didn't even remember ever having read a complete book on my own besides Bobby Twin books. So I started that very night. I began the first paragraph, and I was amazed. I did not want to put it down. Every available time all weekend long I read this story. I read about this girl that was so much like me and yet she lived in a different country at a different time. I felt all the things that she was feeling, the loneliness, the need for somebody who could really listen and understand me. It was at that time that I probably started becoming ready to be an English teacher, a lover of literature and a lover of writing.

I had started reading the Bible at around 11 years old. Our preacher at church, Brother Bryant, saw me respond at a revival when he said, "If any of you are not sure of the state of your soul with the Lord, raise your hand.” I did, because I wasn’t sure how I was supposed to feel. Then, the next afternoon, Brother Bryant came to our house and told my Dad he wanted to talk with me. I was in the orchard wearing shorts and a halter top, a homemade stretch top with two pieces of elastic, one at the bottom, one at the top. I was so embarrassed. I felt I was not fully dressed. I had embarrassed my folks in front of Brother Bryant years before when he had just started at our church. At that time I was about 8 or 9 years old, and it had been our turn to ask the preacher and his family to have dinner (lunch actually) after church with us. People took turns inviting the paster and his family to Sunday dinner after church. Mother made the perfect dinner, and we were eating when I said, "Brother Bryant, do you know what happened to the little boy who lost his gum in the chicken yard?" and he said, "No, what happened to him?" I smiled and said, "He thought he found it three times, but he didn't." Mother was so humiliated that I would tell a joke about chewing chicken poop! So, I definitely did not want to embarrass us all again. He just smiled and asked if I had questions about growing into a young woman. I knew what he meant, and then I was the one who was embarrassed. I just told him I wanted to understand the Bible better, so he suggested I start reading it every day. He said I would find my answers there. So I determined to read the whole Bible, and I did, though I could never say I fully understood.

Soon I began to realize that reading was an outlet, a gift, a means to greater understanding and self-growth, a doorway to more.

Carol Siskovic's mother-in-law, Anne Siskovic Kuhar, gave this picture to Carol because she said it reminded her of Carol and her love of literature.

Balance, Balance, Balance

Alliteration can be musical, beautiful,
or tiring, needlessly repetitive.
Like life!

So, we find ourselves switching
from one end of the spectrum
to the other.

Days when we desire, even pine for,
hours and hours of nothingness
free of requirements.

When the "lack of" begins to bore into us,
we change, desiring, yes-needing activity,
purpose, a feeling of worth!

Both boredom and "boar"dom prove necessary!
Both unbothered lounging and
fierce pointed aiming toward goals.

We must beat up on, defeat, any sign of uselessness!
Or something within us sickens, may die.
Balance proves best.

Dreary days enhance efforts.
Dreamy drifting perfects planning.
Results radiate.

Life is learning, learning, always learning.
Sensing when to shift, when to
"Boar the Boredom."

Carol M. Siskovic

9

Though Murlyn Spurry's death hit me hard, the saddest year of my life was my ninth grade year in high school. I was 14 and 15. It all started right after Christmas. My mother and dad were the type who never shared any problems with their children and didn't let us know what was going on. So I had no idea that they were extremely worried that they were going to lose their house and land. They were so proud of owning their own place. They had made the downpayment, and the rest had been on a loan. They had to make the yearly payment when the crops came in. It was always said that "if you had three bad years in the South, farming cotton, that you were done for," and that apparently is what happened to my folks. They had had three years of bad crops.

They had to move away because they could not make the payment and keep up the loan without a new job. So I found out right after Christmas that my dad had secured a position with the help of my Uncle Roy. Daddy was going to work for a big planter who had thousands of acres, and he was going to manage some of the farms for him. He would also be able to live in the back of a store, and he and Mother together could run the store and make extra money. So, at the end of the year, they had arranged to move out of the Pal Place and move into the back of that store. Daddy would start working for that plantation owner.

They had also made an arrangement with my sister who had been married since the age of 18. She and her husband, Paul Broadway, worked in Clarksdale and were renting a house there. So they agreed that they would come and live in the Pal Place with me so that I could finish out the school year at Clarksdale High School in ninth grade. They would get the rent free, but they had to travel the 12 miles back and forth to Clarksdale every day to work and come home. They had to see after me, and the plan was that I would finish the year, then possibly change schools, or do another year living in our house with Jean and Paul and my nephew Terry. The situation didn't bother me that much, but I didn't understand why it was happening. I liked the idea of living with Jean and Paul and Terry, and life went on pretty much as usual. Except on the weekends, when my mother and dad or somebody else would come get me and take me to stay with them for the two days. Jean and Paul would be on their own for the weekend. That plan went on all Spring long.

In April, my brother Thomas got a furlough from the army. He had taught as a coach the previous year at Crenshaw High School and had fallen in love with Lucy Goodman, a senior at the school. When he left teaching and went into the army, they continued to write, and he asked her to marry him when he came home in April, so we all went to the wedding at the end of April. She was to graduate from high school in May. Thomas went back to the base where he was stationed, and he and his bride would live together after she graduated. Then in May, Jean and my mother picked me up after school, and we were going to Lucy's graduation since she was our new sister-in-law and new daughter-in-law. After school, we headed from Clarksdale to Marks, Mississippi, and from Marks would cut up north toward Crenshaw to go to the high school graduation.

Just before we got to Marks, we were driving along a two lane highway, and we had no seatbelts at that time. Cars didn't have them then. I was sitting in the back and had my arms propped on the front bench seat between Jean who was driving and my mother sitting beside her. As I leaned on that seat, we were talking. In front of us, a car had pulled off on the side of the highway and stopped. It was obviously letting somebody out, but we didn't pay any attention. That often happened on a two-lane highway. Another car was coming toward us, and just as we approached the back of the parked car, a little girl under age six ran out right in front of us and looked up. She saw our car and stopped, frozen in place on the road. As soon as my sister saw her, she hit the brakes with all her might. I was holding on like crazy to keep from being thrown forward. My sister was holding on to the steering wheel, and my mother was hanging on to whatever she could grab. We couldn't stop, and we couldn't hit the car headed toward us or the parked car. No way to avoid the child! I watched the girl's terrified face coming toward us as we hit her.

I heard the scraping of the brakes and watched the expression on her face as she realized that a car was going to hit her. The hit tossed her up in the air, and she came hurtling toward the windshield and came right across the top of the car and off to the side. Then our car suddenly came to a stop, and it seemed like we all jumped out at the same time. Each one of us later thought we were the first to get to the little girl. She was obviously dead. All the people were screaming and yelling. The mother who had been in the front seat of the two-door car blamed herself because she had opened her door. The little girl had been in the backseat in the days of no seatbelts. She had squeezed behind her mother's seat and run around in front of the car because she was so eager to get to her home across the highway. Nobody was able to catch her and stop her.

That whole night was just miserable. My sister kept saying "I'd rather it had been my own child than somebody else's." Her own child, Terry, was two and a half at the time and just the sweetest little boy in the world. We all loved him so much. After that tragedy, there was so much sadness in the house that it was an awful two weeks to get through until school ended when I moved in with my parents behind the store for the summer. Just two weeks into the summer, early one morning, the phone rang, and I was barely conscious of it. My dad answered it, and all of a sudden, he screamed out. I had never heard him scream like that. "Terry is dead. Oh God, Terry's dead!" We got together really fast, pulled our clothes together, jumped in the car, and headed to the Pal Place. All the way, we hardly talked, and I was just trying to figure out what might have happened.

The story was that my sister had put Terry to bed after Prayer Meeting, and he'd had a terrible cough. She had given him cough syrup, and the people who kept him during the day had given him cough syrup all day long. It was adult cough syrup, and it must have put him into a deep sleep. At four o'clock in the morning Jean woke up hearing a voice in her head, "Check your baby. Check Terry." She looked at him and he was okay. So she lay her head back down, and again she heard that voice: "I said check Terry now." She reached over and touched him, and he was ice cold. He was dead. She started screaming, and she picked him up and then both Paul and Jean went crazy. Both of them were running outside with Terry, still wearing night clothes. There was a young man named James Howard who worked for the place, and he was up early milking the cows and feeding the animals and everything. This was about five o'clock in the morning, and he saw they were running to the car in their sleeping attire - Paul in his underwear, Jean in her gown. He ran and grabbed clothes for them and threw them in the car as they got in and raced like crazy, heading to Clarksdale for the hospital. They almost passed Dr. Ballard's house, but pulled in yelling for him. Dr. Ballard was the doctor that had delivered everybody or at least been at the birth of everybody in that community, including mine. He came out when the horn was blowing and checked the baby. He said, "No, he's dead. He's already dead. He's been dead for a while. He's cold." But Paul could not accept it. He said "No, no, he's not. I'm going on to Clarksdale." And so he took off, and a preacher from nearby, James Fortenberry, a young man in his early 20s, went with them. They made it to Clarksdale, but, of course, Terry had been dead for quite a while.

It was an awful, awful experience. And the next few days, the next few weeks, the next few months were terrible. We thought things couldn't get much worse.

About six weeks later, we learned that our Pal Place home had burned in the night. Jean and Paul hadn't been able to bear staying where Terry had died, so Daddy had rented the house out to somebody and moved furniture and belongings into one room that he had locked. When he stopped by in a few weeks to check things, he found some items had been stolen. So he felt he had to ask the new tenants to leave. The house was not being lived in at the time of the fire. Nobody knew if the former renters had set the fire. Another possibility was that a man who had wanted to buy the land for his own had made it impossible for the owner to return any time soon.

Either way, my mother and father had worked so many years to buy their own place and spent so many years making it nice. They considered it their lifetime house and had intended to come back to it soon. But now, it had burned to the ground. At that time, they felt there just wasn't much else that could go wrong in their lives.

It was what I call "The Summer I Grew up." I learned what it was to survive all kinds of tragedies. I grew up and, as hard as it was, it gave me the strength to go forward. If I could survive all that, I could do about anything.

Carol, 13 almost 14, with Terry a year before Terry's death on June 4, 1954. Carol Malone, Bethanne Malone, Terry Broadway, Ronnie Malone, Donna Parker (Aunt Doad's granddaughter)

Paul and Jean Broadway went on to have two healthy children who grew to adulthood, Trudy and Randy, circa mid 1960s.

Terry

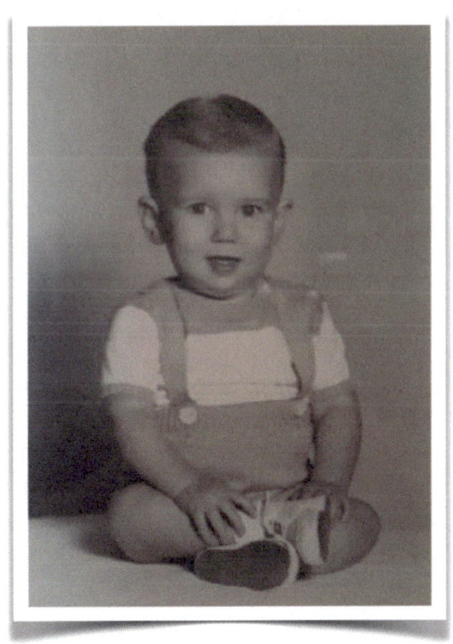

Terry Broadway

When All Is Lost

The key word is LOST.
It implies some things found.
Life rewards treasured, valuable,
irreplaceable, truly profound.

Not just persons or items of worth,
but a part that made a whole,
a completion, an achievement,
the attainment of a life goal.

Now, a different "together" exists,
for the mind and soul can not let go.
That special love may seem removed, gone,
but we never lose what we truly came to know.

We've become embedded, soaked,
possessed through and through
by what fully blessed us, and now…
the "all" refines — spiritual and new.

Loss saddens, changes us, and perhaps,
if we allow, will bring us hope, not stress.
Such a miracle when less becomes more,
when grief finds a way to lift up, to bless!

Gain and loss, the game of life,
forever seeking each day's ideal,
while trying to empty an ocean of strife
with a small cup and resilient will.

Carol M. Siskovic

Like Quick-footed Animals

All the parts of the calendar
push forward relentlessly.
Even when the movement
appears to slow, it passes
in smooth thundering continuity.
Whether drawn forward by
something enticing out there,
or pushed by an unknown
force from behind, stopping
or pausing is no alternative.
Chase or race or be doomed.
Head up into the wind, heart
heaving and hooves hefting,
the present body blasts time.
In this form in this moment
in this life, breath must quicken
until the last slow exhalation.
Until the final step on solid ground.
Until the soul rises on its own,
enters that realm that feels right.

Carol M. Siskovic

10

When I was young, I didn't get to travel much. Most of the time, traveling meant going to church on Sunday from our house to Cagle's Crossroads Community Church, called Union Chapel. And that was just a few miles. Or we would go to Clarksdale on Saturdays, only 12 miles away. We would also go to Tutwiler to the Tutrovansum movie theater on Friday night or Saturday night, and that was like four or five miles, not far at all.

Where you start your life probably makes a permanent imprint and stays with you always. But I think I was in seventh grade before I first felt the need to really get outside my well-known zone. It became apparent to me in the seventh grade that if I was going to do anything different in my life, to get off the farm, and not spend my life doing farm work, picking and chopping cotton, tending chickens, and all of that, I probably needed a better education. I knew that, supposedly, the people in the nearby town of Clarksdale, Mississippi, got a better education and were better off than the farm people out in the country.

A lot of people from Dublin had gone to Clarksdale and finished school there, especially if they were good at sports. They were tempted to play on a big town team, and my brother had thought that he would do that. That's when I guess I first became really aware of it. Thomas, who was eight years older than I, decided that he would go play football in Clarksdale and go to school there. But he didn't stay. He started the football season, but he just didn't feel comfortable with the guys that he had not grown up with and didn't know. Thomas didn't feel as capable and included as he had felt at Dublin. Even before actual school started, he decided that Clarksdale High School was not for him. He told Mother and Daddy, "Nope, I'm going to Dublin. I'm going to finish from Dublin."

I had remembered that. So, I thought, "If I go to Clarksdale, I can't be quitting like that. If I make up my mind to do it, then I have to do it." I talked to my mother and said, "I think I'd like to go to Clarksdale High School." She said, "Well, you know we have to pay for the bus to pick you up. It'll be $12 a month." And that was almost like saying it would be $2,000 a month now. I think it was a lot coming up with 12 extra dollars every month. It was not going to be easy for her. So she said she'd talk it over with Daddy. And she did. They decided that if I really wanted to, they would do it.

So just before eighth grade, I went to Clarksdale, and I took the necessary tests, went through the enrollment, and arranged for the bus to pick me up. It was not easy to make changes like that. But I did manage to get through, and that was my first real adventure away from the norm. I had never traveled outside my little circle into a bigger circle where I did not feel totally comfortable. But I survived. I knew I could do it, would do it.. Then, later, I had to change schools again, and I graduated from West Tallahatchie High School. That was because we had to move when our house burned.

Before I even started to West Tallahatchie, I got an opportunity to travel outside the state other than just over the state border to Memphis, Tennessee, which wasn't really considered going outside our comfort zone. That was still part of the Mississippi Delta as far as we were concerned. But my brother Thomas had married in the spring of the year, was in the army, and had been transferred to Paducah, Kentucky. So, in the summer before I entered 11th grade, I finally took my first long trip to visit Thomas and Lucy who had just had a baby. He and Lucy lived there in a small apartment. My mother and dad and I went to see the new baby, and my parents left me for a week, they said to help Thomas and Lucy. My brother was working, and Lucy was at home taking care of the new baby. I proved to be very little help to them, and the only thing I did while I was staying there was go with the neighbors down to Kentucky Lake one afternoon and stand on the beach. I didn't even go swimming. I put my toes in the water, but that was about it. Then when my parents came to pick me up, they brought Jean and Paul, my sister and my brother-in-law. I didn't see a lot on that visit, but I realized that I was in a different state and experiencing new things.

On the way back home, we went through Nashville, and we attended the Grand Ole Opry, which was one of the first big shows that I ever got to attend. I wasn't even a fan of country music at that time. But I really did enjoy it. That was, at that time, the biggest thing I had ever done in my whole life; to go to Nashville to the Ryman Auditorium and to see the Grand Ole Opry. It put the bug in me. I wanted to see more. I wanted to know more about the world. I wanted to see different places, so after that, every opportunity I ever got to travel, I would take.

The next bit of traveling I did was at the end of my senior year in high school. The boy that I was dating, Billy Gardner, was going every summer to work with his sister and brother-in-law in the Washington DC area in a little town in Maryland. I had graduated, but Billy still had another year to go even though we were the same age; he had started later. At the end of the summer his mother and father were driving there to pick him up, so they invited me to travel with them. And I did, even though I didn't relish traveling in the car with his parents for I don't know how many hours, all that long way. After all, it meant traveling and seeing Washington DC. I sat in the back of their car as we traveled across the states. We started early in the morning, drove all day long and got there late at night. This was my first real venture away from family. We visited with his sister's family for a few days and then drove back. But even then, they didn't show me a lot. They took me to downtown DC to a department store; that's what the mother wanted to do. I wanted to see the sights so they just pointed out the things that we passed as we went to that department store. The big deal for me was seeing the Lincoln Memorial, the capitol, and the White House as we drove past them. That trip did help ready me to actually leave home and travel away to college to live .

After working at Yellowstone, finishing college, getting my masters, and teaching for four years, I decided I had enough money to go traveling in Europe. I had survived a pretty damaging auto accident and had received a pretty good settlement so I had the cash and the time before changing jobs and moving from my teaching job in Gulfport,

Mississippi, to a new teaching position in Dallas, Texas. It was the perfect time for European traveling. A friend, Harriet Stanley, and I decided to take the money that we had saved up and to spend the entire summer traveling all over Europe. And that's what we did. We began our trip by flying from New Orleans to DC and then on to London, England. We had purchased a EURAIL pass which covered all European buses and trains for the summer so we were able to move easily from England to France, Brussels, Denmark, Germany, Switzerland, Austria, Italy, Greece, and Spain, from where we flew back to New Orleans in late August.

On my return from England, I moved from Mississippi to Dallas, Texas, to start my new teaching job with Highland Park High School, and join my two roommates, Betty Tynes and Lois Lawson. In October, I reconnected with Joel Siskovic who had been transferred from Keesler AFB to the base in San Angelo, Texas. The following April he was transferred to Clark AFB in the Philippines.

The summer after he left, I traveled to Connecticut where I met Joel's family and then on to Burlington, Vermont, where I attended a summer Institute in Elizabethan
Arts and Literature. My two roommates joined me in August, and we toured the eastern states from Vermont to South Carolina, then returned to Dallas for the next teaching year.

At the beginning of May in that year, I received my surprise, middle-of-the-night telephone call from Joel in the P.I. He said he was catching a plane back to Texas and asked me to marry him! Quite a shock! And calling for fast decisions and imminent changes.

I had to plan for a trip in July to the Philippine Islands where we would live during the first part of our marriage. From the Philippines, we came back to Mississippi and then to Texas, and then to Maryland, and then four years in England. While we were in England, we did a lot of traveling and then finally came back to Texas and settled in San Antonio, Texas. So I was fortunate to be able to travel a lot during young adulthood, to see so much of the world. To this day I enjoy traveling and still will travel every chance I get.

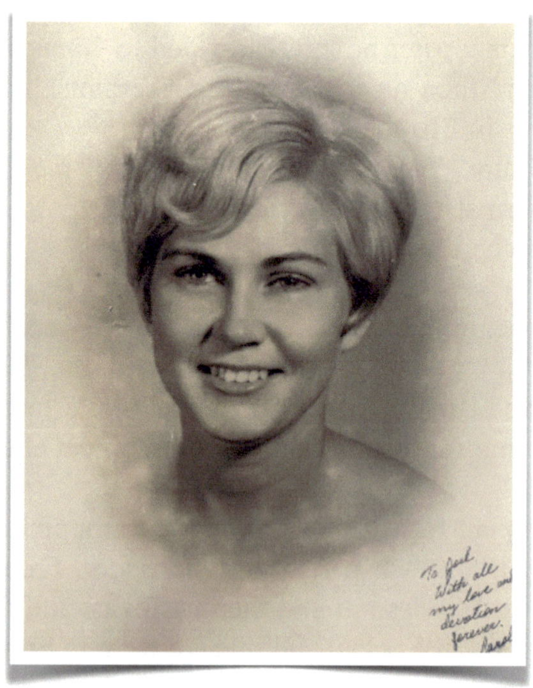

Young Adult Years

I Am Green

Not like early leaves on spring twigs.
Not like those first sprigs of grass peaking
from soil trying to overcome winter ravages.
Not like the lime freshness of a Raspa,
that shaved ice treat so tempting and cool.
Nor like happy body paint on St. Paddy's Day.

I can still remember my mother's warning,
"You don't want to grow up to be green!"
It made no sense. Everyone knew
a green apple was not yet ready so
wasn't she fearing the impossible.
Grown up meant you were ripe.

Her caution would have meant much more
if she'd said, "Don't grow up to be eaten!"
Funny, because here I am, a ripe old age
and literally eaten alive by how little I know.
Finally with time to devote myself to learning,
I vividly understand how little time I have left.

And how extremely green I still am!

Carol M. Siskovic

Where the Waters Take Us

Not always by choice
we find ourselves midstream,
heading out and away
toward a perceived goal,
sometimes floating,
often lunging and sweeping
seeking something out there…
a longed-for landing,
a desired destination,
a glorious goal or gift.
In seas calm or stormy,
crowded or solitary, we must
forge forward undaunted,
pursuing our raison d'être.

Carol M. Siskovic

11

After out house burned down, Mother and Daddy were anxious to rcplace their home and to find a good place to live. They kept the store at Blue Lake for another year, and then in the middle of my 11th grade year, we moved. Daddy got the chance to buy a store in the country outside Minter City, Mississippi, with a house attached, and with a little bit of land. After he sold the land from the Pal Place, he had a little money to make a down payment. So even without showing the place to Mother or to me, he came home and said he had found a new place for us to live. Mother, of course, was very doubtful. When we went there and saw the narrow little house attached to a plain store, she was so disappointed. It didn't even come close to matching the beauty of the home that had burned down, but we moved in, and we adjusted. At least it was theirs, and Home.

That was the middle of my junior year in high school, and I started going to Minter City to catch the bus to West Tallahatchie High School. That way, I didn't have to change high schools. I was already very concerned about how I could go to college as Mother and Daddy had no extra money. I knew I was going to college somewhere, but I thought I would have to go to a junior college for two years and try to earn money and pay my way as I went. I just didn't know. So I went to the school counselor who also just happened to be the school's coach. I said, "Is there any way I can get a scholarship for college?" and he said, "What do you need a scholarship for? You can get a job as a secretary, or you could go to nursing school, but you'll probably get married and just be a housewife, right?" And I said, "I hope not. I really want to go to college." Then he replied, "Well… I'll see what I can find."

A few weeks later, he called me back to his office and proudly announced, "I found something called the CM Gooch Scholarship Fund out of Memphis. and here's the information. You can send off and get the forms to apply for this if you want to try it." That's all he knew, so I did it. I wrote a letter that said that I would like to apply for the fund, and I filled out the papers and got my grades sent, and all that was required. I finally received notice that I needed to do an interview with a representative of Gooch, and that the nearest representative for me to have an appointment with was a principal of Rosedale, a school about an hour away.

Jean came down and picked me up and took me for the interview that had been assigned to me. I missed school that day and at the interview the principal was apparently impressed since he sent back a positive interview recommendation. About a month later, I got information that I had been awarded the CM Gooch Scholarship to the college of my choice. The first year tuition would be fully paid; after that I would be given a loan for the following years, which I would have to repay at a rate that was satisfactory to both of us. So I knew then that I could go to the school of my choice. Right around that time, the preacher of Minter City Methodist Church, who had gone to Millsaps College in Jackson, Mississippi, wanted to take a few of us from the church to High School Day at Millsaps. We went with him, and had a wonderful time. There were three of us who went, and we all ended up at Millsaps, the other two starting one and two years after me. As soon as I got to Millsaps, it just felt so comfortable and right that I knew I had chosen correctly. To this day, I feel that that choice has made a definite difference in my life in so many ways.

It was a beautiful campus, and all the students were working and greeting everybody, and they were so nice. I thought almost immediately, “This is where I want to go." We ended our day attending a beautiful production of “South Pacific” that night. Everything had been so impressive, and then during that play I thought, “This is the most fantastic thing to be able to go to school and to see beautiful theater like this.” On our way home, I told my pastor, whose name, ironically, was Brother Millsaps, “I really want to go to Millsaps College!” so he smiled and then did everything he could to help me. All Mother and Daddy had to do was come up with living expenses like money for food for me. The tuition and dormitory was paid by the scholarship for the first year. Then the loan for the rest I was able to pay back at a rate of my choosing. After six years of teaching, I had paid back all my loan, plus contributions to a much-appreciated scholarship fund.

My first year, I also decided to go out for Rush. I had been invited to an early overnight party by one of the sororities, and I thought I would try Rush just to get to know people. I did not know anything about sororities or how to get recommendations, and, of course, was not taken in by any of the popular ones. But a smaller sorority, Beta Sigma Omicron, gave me a bid. I asked Mother if if there was any way that they could give me $65 for the yearly fees. She said she would find it, so I joined that sorority. I didn't know it at the time, but I was making lifelong friendships. Some of my best friends today I met at that sorority, and it was a wonderful four years. There are a number of us who still keep in touch after over half a century, even though we live in different states and long distances apart. Thank goodness for modern forms of communication!

At the beginning of my second college year, I was called into the college President’s office. I was terrified. Why would I be called to the Presidents office? I was just told what time to come, and I went. I was shown into the office, and I sat down nervously. President Finger said, “Well, I called you in here, Miss Malone, for a very important reason." I thought, "Oh, my goodness.! What did I do wrong?" Then he smiled and said, "I am informing you that your second year of college has already been fully paid." I said, "By Gooch?" He replied, "No, the Gooch Foundation will be loaning you nothing this year. It's fully paid." I asked, "Who…who…who gave it to me?" He responded, "It's been requested that I not reveal the donor. But it was someone who wanted to make sure that you had a second year of college." So that year was paid for also, and I never learned who to thank. It made me think constantly that I might be talking to or seeing my donor, which makes you more appreciative to almost everyone!

When I finished college, Mother and Daddy and Thomas and Lucy came to see my graduation, and as we were all riding back in the car afterwards, Thomas asked Daddy what I would be doing all summer." I spoke up and said "I don't have any plans." He told Daddy (not me), "If I were you, I would just sign her up at Ole Miss and let her get started on her Masters. And Daddy answered, "I guess I could do that." I knew that was what I wanted to do, but Mother had already written to me and told me I needed to get a job. So I wasn't going to ask them to pay for anything. That night, before I went to bed, Daddy said, "Get up early tomorrow, and I will take you to Oxford (where Ole Miss was located). That's how I knew he would pay for my summer school. So we picked up Thomas the next morning, and he helped me get enrolled and signed up for summer housing. In the ten weeks before I started teaching, I got 12 hours toward my Masters degree. Then the Friday before I had to start teaching on Monday, my Mother and I drove to Clarksdale so I could find a place to live. I still cannot believe I chanced waiting so long before finding a place to live!

Carol Malone

1960
Alpha Zeta Chapter
of
Beta Sigma Omicron
1961

Off to School Again

The dog taught me to walk,
patiently allowed my clinging,
climbing and slow giggly steps
until I found balance and toddled
off to leave him behind, watching.

All my teachers, in my memory,
line up behind that patient dog,
each serving my life, then
checking my progress a while
before we moved on and apart.

Each day school begins anew,
all creatures, sights, happenings
bringing their separate lessons.
Many, just necessary reviews. Others,
lightening strikes, aromatic blossoms.

Some, as sweet as the kiss of a dog.

Carol Siskovic

12

When I began my teaching career, it was not my first working experience. During my high school senior Christmas vacation, I took a job as a cashier for a five-and-dime store at Drew, Mississippi, only a short drive from our Minter City home. I learned one very important lesson during those few weeks: I never, ever wanted to work full time as a clerk or sales person! I had long ago determined during my various farm experiences that I never wanted to do farm work, and I wasn't even sure that I had what it took to do simple gardening of any kind. Later during my Sophomore and Junior year in college, when I was 21, I worked at Yellowstone National Park with two other girls from Millsaps. We sent our applications never expecting that we would be accepted. My friends, both in another sorority, got a job at Fishing Bridge, which was one of many Yellowstone work locations. But my job was at Old Faithful. We weren't going to be working together, but at least we could travel together. So they picked up the train in Jackson, Mississippi, and I caught the same train at Grenada, Mississippi. My mother and dad had allowed me to take the job, and they took me to Grenada to catch the train. I boarded and kept walking until I found my friends, and the three of us rode that train all the way to Chicago. We got off but had a while before we had to catch another train later that evening. We had all afternoon long to walk around in downtown Chicago and see all that we could see. That was the farthest I had ever been from home, and we had at least that far to continue to Montana.

We saw the department stores, of course, big stores unlike those in Mississippi. And then we went to an art museum and spent hours. We saw everything we could see within walking distance of the train station. We didn't have money for a taxi or anything, and we didn't want to chance getting too far away. That evening we got back on the train and began our ride across the upper United States, all the way to Bozeman, Montana. That's where we separated because there had been hundreds of kids on that train going to work in Yellowstone. We all unloaded, and there were big buses there from the various places in Yellowstone. They announced: "All of you people line up at the place where you go to work. Look for the sign that says your place." That's when I said goodbye to my friends. I was standing there, not knowing anybody. They said to look around for anybody you want as a roommate. I looked around, and there was a girl standing next to me, and she looked at me. She said "Do you have a roommate?" I said, "No, I don't." She responded, "I don't either. You want to be roommates?" So we agreed and then exchanged names. When she said her name was Carol, I said, "That's my name too!" Her name was Carol Turner, and I was Carol Malone. She was from Florida and I from Mississippi, both far from home and both assigned to work at the Old Faithful cafeteria.

We became roommates, and we worked together all summer. Together, we got to travel and see many areas of Montana and Wyoming. We workers all got one day off a week. We would go out early in the morning and stand on the highway. People would be traveling to and fro, and they knew that the young people needed rides. So if they stopped, we'd ask them where they were going and then decide if we wanted to go where they were going. By hitchhiking with vacationers, we got to tour the surrounding areas. We would usually travel in twos or threes. It never could be more than that because there wouldn't be room in a car to hitch a ride.

But that way, on our days off, we got to see inside the park and all around it. Toward the end of our summer in 1959, there was one of the biggest earthquakes there that had ever been in all of the United States. It was just really scary. Huge rocks tumbled down onto highways, crashing into cars, and some buildings fell. One mountain top outside the town of Yellowstone fell into a lake, and the lake water was permanently moved to a different location, covering a much-traveled highway. But I was at Old Faithful, and the only thing that happened at Old Faithful was that all the gas lines broke and the electricity went out. So we were never in much danger. They stopped most of the traffic at that time. Then they started closing a lot of the sites, and they said anybody who wanted to go home could go home early. Those workers who wanted to finish out the summer would move into the places that were open.

So my roommate and I were moved from Old Faithful to Yellowstone Lake Inn. "The Two Carols," spent the last few weeks of the summer at the Lake and served people at the restaurant there. Then we finally were taken to the train and rode the train together to Chicago and then down to Memphis. She changed trains to go to Florida, and I stayed on the train and went back to Grenada where my mom and dad picked me up. That was the first big trip of my life, many more to come.

The next summer, I did the same thing and went back to Yellowstone, this time to work as a waitress at Old Faithful Restaurant, one of the fanciest eating places in the park. I didn't think that my friend from Florida, the other Carol, was coming back as I hadn't kept in touch. When I got back to Old Faithful, I was assigned a new roommate. I went to the restroom and, lo and behold, there were my two friends from Florida. And we were surprised to meet other friends of ours in the restaurant later. There we all were! Together again.

Being a waitress was much different from working in a cafeteria line as I had the summer before. It required a lot more time, attention to detail, accuracy, and congeniality. But the tips made it all worthwhile. And the Matre d' tried to be fair in his distribution of big parties, probable heavy tippers, and well-known personalities. The most notable person that I served that summer was a New York state supreme court judge with his family. It turned out that my best tips for the summer came because complaints were made about slow service, and the Matre d' was very brusk with me. I was given a table of five couples for breakfast, and each person made a completely different order. The kitchen was slow on specialized orders, and we had been instructed not to serve anyone at a table until all the orders could be served. So I was in the kitchen trying to get the cooks and staff to get all the orders complete. Meanwhile, the couples were anxious to get their touring started, plus they were hungry. So they complained vociferously to the Matre d', and he loudly came into the kitchen after me, yelling at everyone and grabbing whatever foods and extra staff were available to bring out multiple trays. I was trying to serve the orders correctly, but he was simply grabbing a plate and saying, "Who wants this (and he would call out whatever was on the plate). I got so upset with all the frantic hubbub that tears started rolling down my cheeks. The waitress uniform was a dress with a matching apron with huge pockets, and I began to notice that my apron pockets were starting to feel so heavy. That's when I noticed that the women and a few men were dropping silver dollars in my pocket as I served and passed by. Part of the fun of being at Yellowstone was receiving and collecting silver dollars as change when purchasing things in the park. So they were trying to make things better for me with good tips. We finally got a plate or several plates to everyone, with minimal charge, and got them all on their way, muttering soft "sorry"s as they left. A really uncomfortable situation with a truly comfortable ending!

My friend, Carol, had met her future husband who was also working at Yellowstone and by summer's end, he, Jim Hill, decided to drive us all home, going all the way from Montana to Florida to meet his future in-laws. The four of us made that cross-country trip in August, seeing many interesting sights along the way. In Kansas City, we took time to see an outdoor amphitheater presentation of "Westside Story," even better than the movie which came out later. They finally dropped me off in Memphis, and we said goodby, for what turned out to be forever. Then my brother, Gwin, who lived in Memphis, drove me home to begin my final year of college.

That was the beginning of my many travels, and from then on I took every opportunity I could to go to new places. I took one summer after I had taught for four years and traveled all over Europe. Then, later on, I traveled around Asia after Joel and I married and were living in the Philippines. During that assignment, we traveled to Thailand, Taiwan, and Hong Kong, and later went to China, Japan, and Alaska.

Seven years later, we were stationed in England from which we traveled into Scotland, Ireland, Germany, France, and Israel. I went to Russia at one time alone because Joel and all those who worked in intelligence were not allowed to go there. In fact, I put together a tour group with the Air Force wives, and we went to Moscow, St Petersburg/ Leningrad and surrounding areas. That was quite an experience because Russia was pretty much a closed country at that time. During my earlier summer abroad before we had married, I had experienced a brief tour from Wast Berlin through the Wall to East Communist Berlin. It had been like traveling from day to night, from loud, busy happiness to dark, quiet imprisonment. So, I expected a different atmosphere in Russia, and things were not so dark, but there was definitely a constant feeling of care.

After trips to France, Scotland, Ireland, and Israel, we returned to the states after four years abroad. Years later, without Joel, I went on tours to Portugal, Spain, and China. I have not yet toured in Africa, Australia, or Antarctica. I have been to South America, but only on cruises when Joel and I took short tours off the ship. Naturally, living in San Antonio, we dipped into Mexico a bit but never much, and never to Mexico City.

There is still a lot of traveling I'd like to do. Of course, I've never been to the moon, but I may have to save that one for another lifetime!

Old Faithful Inn, Entrance Drive
Library of Congress Prints and Photographs Division
https://www.loc.gov/resource/hhh.wy0093.photos/?sp=19

What a Poem Is Not

Not a proof of intelligence or talent.
Not a guarantee of longevity or loveliness.

No insurance of ease in writing, understanding,
No definite connection with all, or anyone else.
No assurance of a sense of completion.

Never a waste of time, no matter who judges.
Never lacking a degree of catharsis.
Never without vibrations of enjoyment, satisfaction.
Never never ever less than a child born of the heart.

As a moth drawn to hot light, a poem must
do what it does, be what it is; it cannot seek safety.
It wants to please, but it never depends on approval.
It cannot become for praise or reward.
The saddest negative is a poem felt, but not written.

Carol M. Siskovic

Full Sky

Everything you own
exposed to an uncaring
world.

How you
got here to this life-
your story- might seem dull, unworthy, to many,
and may prove unlasting in the universal
collection of millions and millions,
but….

Each story,
including yours, shines
in its solitary
location, its lonely position in an endless
sky of individualistic, authentic
stars.

Whether
seen or overlooked,
smiled upon,
or not, remembered, forgot, each
body radiates its
singular worth in an amazing,
endlessly beautiful
universe.

Carol M. Siskovic

Teaching

13

Back when I finished college, I had hoped that I would receive a scholarship to the University of Arkansas. The head of the English department at Millsaps had promised me his full recommendation, and he said that for many years he had decided on one person who would be recommended by him and always was accepted for the masters program at University of Arkansas. They had never failed to take his recommendation. However, at the beginning of my senior year in college, Dr. White decided to retire and another man took over. When I registered for my second semester classes, the new department head had wanted me to take 18th century literature classes that he was teaching.

I told that professor that since this was Dr. White's last semester to teach that I intended to take Romantic Poets and Victorian Poets under Dr. White (instead of his classes). I could see that he was not pleased by that, but I stuck to my decision and the courses I wanted to take. About two weeks later, Dr. White caught me in the hall one day, and he said "I am so sorry to tell you this, Miss Malone, but you are not going to get the scholarship from the University of Arkansas. I was informed that they always give the scholarship to a person recommended by the head of the English department …and I'm no longer the department head. The new department head does not want to recommend you." The professor whose classes I refused to take had refused to recommend someone who wouldn't take his advice. I had brought that on myself without realizing how it would affect me. The sad thing was that no one from Millsaps got that scholarship that year.

I did not receive the recommendation, and therefore did not get the scholarship, so after graduation I did not know what I was going to do. My mother said they didn't have the money to pay for me to go to graduate school, and that I definitely needed to get a job. They had "done all they could do." I told my good friend Betty Lou Times, and she told her father who had been the superintendent of schools at West Tallahatchie when I graduated from high school, and knew me well. He sent me a letter saying that when I graduated he had a job for me if I wanted to take it, and I wrote him back immediately and said "yes." I definitely needed a job so he hired me to teach eighth grade English for the Clarksdale Public Schools where he was presently in charge as Superintendent.

When I graduated, I didn't know what I was going to do for the summer, and my brother Thomas probably did the nicest thing he ever did for me on the way home when he told Daddy, "What you really need to do is to come up with the money and get her started working on her masters at Ole Miss. You can start her with the first payment, and if she's working she'll be able to make the other payments." Daddy said that sounded like something they could do. By Monday afternoon I was enrolled in a masters course for the summer before my first year of teaching.

I completed 12 hours toward my Masters Degree. Then, I think two or three days before school was to begin, I came home. My mother and I went to Clarksdale, and we searched for a place for me to live, but I couldn't find one anywhere. I went to the school office to see Mr. Tynes and told him that maybe I'd waited too long to find a place to live. He said, "Well, interestingly enough, the school owns a house right next to the campus where you will be teaching. Mrs. Belk who rents it from us, is renting individual rooms and apartments. Why don't you go see if she has a room to spare." That is exactly what I did. I went to her house immediately and told her that Mr. Tines had told me to come see her and ask if she had a room to rent.

She took me upstairs and showed me an absolutely huge room with two single beds in it and nice furniture and a nice overlook of the street. When I asked her how much the room would be, she said "$25 a month." I responded immediately, "I'll take it!" She said, "Fine, when will I see you?" I told her I'd move in Sunday afternoon. I was so happy. I had a place to live!

Over the weekend, I got all my stuff together, and after church on Sunday, Mother and Daddy drove there with me. They had bought me a car with a $450 down payment prior to that. It was a used Ford Fairlane with a Continental tire kit on the back, which my mother said looked very "tacky." I thought it looked very sporty. I drove that car to Clarksdale, and Mother and Daddy followed me to make sure I got there and got settled. I went in, told Mrs. Belk I was there and introduced her to my parents. She said, "Let me show you to your room," and she took us up to the room with each of us holding clothes or luggage. She knocked on the door, which I thought was peculiar, then opened the door and walked in. Then she said, "And this is your roommate."

Across the room there was a girl sitting on the other cot, and she stared at me, and I stared at her. "This is Gloria Sultan.... Carol Malone.... you are roommates. I'll leave you to get acquainted." She left. and Gloria looked at me, and I was thinking of what to say to her. I was completely bamboozled, and she said, "Before you say anything, let me ask you one question." She asked, "Did you know you had a roommate?" We started laughing so hard. I think we were friends almost immediately. We knew we had been "had," but it was exactly what both of us needed. I don't know how either one of us would've made it without the other during that first year, and that was the beginning of four wonderful years of rooming together.

After two years, we decided we weren't getting enough "action" in this town of Clarksdale. I taught eighth grade and had wonderful students. Gloria taught art to all the elementary students. Both of us were kept working all the time so we decided we needed to seek something else during spring vacation. We drove to the coast and visited some of my college sorority friends, as they were loving their teaching and social life on the coast. They said we were crazy if we didn't get an application to come there too. So we dropped by the school office at Gulfport High School, and both of us got applications and did an interview at that time for a teaching job the next year.. Lo and behold, we both were offered jobs at Gulfport High School. So for the second two years of our teaching careers, Gloria and I taught there. Because Biloxi/Gulfport was the location of Kessler Air Force Base, during our two years there, we dated many Air Force guys. We had a wonderful time and did a lot of good teaching, and we both met our future husbands there. She met Jim Baker and married him in April of 1964, and I met Joel Siskovic and we married in 1967.

When Gloria married, I realized that I probably needed to get a job somewhere else at the same time. She would be living in Florida, and she eventually taught there. I was looking to see what I might do, and I talked with some college friends. One of them was teaching in the Gulfport area, and the other was teaching in the Jackson area. The three of us thought we might like to teach in Texas the next year, so we arranged interviews in the spring of that year. We traveled to Dallas and Houston and did interviews for various jobs. Since Joel had been traveling from Kessler to San Angelo, Texas, I hoped being in Texas would provide chances for reconnection, and it did.

When we went to Dallas, we were actually going to see a friend of ours who was taking courses at SMU in Dallas at that time. After we completed our interviews in the Richardson School System, we were visiting her and her friends. They said that this was a wonderful school district that they were living in called the Highland Park Area, and I said, "Does it have a good high school?" She said, "Yes, it is a wonderful high school!" I asked, "How far is it?" And she said it was just a few blocks away. I decided the next morning when I got up that I would just go down and pick up an application to teach there and see how it went.

I had a beautiful yellow two-piece suit, and I decided to really dress up with high heels. With my hair all done perfectly, I drove to the central office, which was close to the high school. I walked in and went over to the secretary and said, "My name is Carol Malone. I teach in the high school at Gulfport, Mississippi, and I am looking at jobs in this area. I was wondering if I could pick up a job application and maybe fill it out now?" She asked, "What do you teach?" and I told her "English, and I graduated from Millsaps college. I have been teaching for four years now." She said, "Just a moment" because the phone had been ringing. She picked it up and said, "Yes, sir, I'll send her right in." I thought, "What is going on?" and I looked up and there was a door open behind her. The superintendent of the Highland Park Schools had been listening to our conversation. He asked her to send me in. I introduced myself, and he said, "Tell me all about yourself." He asked a number of questions, then said, "I think you will be a perfect fit for us. I'm going to call Mr. Bowlby, the principal of the high school."

Then he talked on the phone and said, "Mr. Bowlby, I'm sending this young lady over, and I want you to interview her right now." He told me, "You only have to go to the other side of the block, park there in front of the high school, go in, and the principal will interview you." I did that, and Mr. Bowlby was very nice. I didn't know how it went, but I was told that I would receive word about my application in a very short time. In just a week or so, not long at all, I received the contract to teach at Highland Park High School. I was absolutely amazed and happy that my two friends received job offers from Richardson Elementary School and were going to be my roommates in Dallas. We spent a very happy two years together teaching in Dallas.

Thank You, Keats

(Sonnet inspired by "On the Grasshopper and Cricket"
by John Keats)

The poetry of earth is never dead:
Each voice that ever spoke or thought to write
Reverberates in space both day and night
Instilling in our souls some word once said.
From sky above to dirt's down deepest bed,
From darkest cloud to sweet renewing light,
Come songs, air gifts, afloat like sailing kites.
And we must look where'er those sounds have led.
The poetry of earth is never ceasing.
Cricket's high chirp to grasshopper's low call,
Soft hum, sharp scream, drumbeats, loved lullaby.
Through life, through death, the stories keep increasing.
Material enough for each, for all,
To capture, save, and share although we die.

Carol M. Siskovic

Words on Paper

Chose an order
Catch the beat
Music demands
Pull it out of the brain
Pull it out of the gut
The Tweetie Bird hammer will guide you
Bang out the goodness
Bang out the badness
no one knows now
and everyone must, soon
can't keep secrets
tap them out, keep the beat
see how it feels
to separate out
parts from parts
thoughts from thoughts
words from words
letters from letters
little breaths connected
like choo choo trains
puffing their way
along new tracks
in spectacular order
watch them as they go.
Now Jump aboard.

Carol M. Siskovic

Travels Continue

14

As told earlier, my travel lust had begun in high school when I first traveled from Memphis to Kentucky and to Nashville and the Grand Ole Opry. It definitely picked up in college when I spent the two summers traveling back and forth to Yellowstone National Park. Now, as I prepared to end the school year at Gulfport, Mississippi, and move on to Dallas, Texas, I was definitely hooked on broadening my horizons.

My college friends and I were all set to make a move to Texas in late August. But now as we approached the end of the school year, I had nothing left to do all summer but kill time, so to speak. I had had an accident the previous year, and in the settlement of the accident, I had come out with about two to three thousand extra dollars. At that time, that amount was more than enough to be able to make a trip abroad. I and a friend, Harriet Stanley, whose mother was a fellow teacher at Gulfport high school, began thinking how we might do something together during the summer. Harriet said, "Why don't we travel around in England or just all over Europe, wherever we want to go this summer, and I said, "That sounds like fun, but can we afford it?" She said, "Sure, we'll just go the cheap route," and we began making our plans. Her mother said, "I don't want you going to Europe for the summer without having certain hotels to be in at certain times," so we picked major cities and got hotel reservations, a few major cities like London, Paris, Brussels, Copenhagen, Zurich, Rome, and Athens. The final one was going to be in Madrid, Spain. We knew that we would make it to those hotels on certain dates, but for the rest of the summer, we didn't know where we were going to be from night to night. Our families would have no idea where we were at any other times. Only where we had been, based on the postcards we sent that always arrived days after we had moved on somewhere else. Needless to say, we had an absolute blast! Every place left us with special memories.

We flew out of New Orleans to DC, and then landed in London. We began our sightseeing from that point. We saw most of London and took tours to Stratford and other points of interest, ending in Canterbury and crossing the channel from there. We also had a Euro Pass that would last us for the summer on boats, buses, and trains, and we spent the whole summer using it. We bought only one airline ticket from Frankfort to Berlin and back. We even managed to arrange a trip into East Berlin, very unusual at that time. We got to see the differences in West Berlin and East Berlin, and it was night and day. It literally felt like moving suddenly from daylight action to dark quiet of night! After flying back from Berlin to Frankfort, we continued all over Europe and Greece. It would take an entire book to tell about everything that we did that summer. All the people we met! All the things that happened to us! It was probably one of the most enlarging experiences of my life. And I later heard that Harriet ended up marrying a man she had met while we were in Zurich. Unfortunately, our lives took separate paths, and we lost touch with each other.

As the summer ended, we flew from Madrid back to New York, spent a few days in New York seeing the sights, then flew back to New Orleans where the Stanleys picked us up. Then I retrieved my car which I'd left at the Stanleys' house and drove home. After a few days, Betty Lou Tynes, Lois Lawson, and I made plans to move to Dallas and begin our first teaching year in Texas. I began the wonderful experience of teaching at Highland Park High School where I remained for the next two years.

A typical Pisa picture but with me!

The Berlin Wall

Volumes

We are not footprints or blueprints
to be followed blindly
by red-shoe feet and white circle eyes
brainlessly plodding and stacking.

We are not yellow-bricked
tree-lined ways to anything emerald
and we become dust to all
tin, straw, lion-like shadows.

We are not numbers beneath
a drawn line or
following an equal sign;
we are the unknowns above, before.

We are a boxful, bagful, headful
of words, just words
that wriggle and jiggle and shake
inside two open hands.

Carol M. Siskovic

Meeting Joel

15

I first met Joel in September of 1964. It was close to Labor Day, and my roommate, Gloria Sultan (now Baker) and I planned to go to the clubs down on the Gulfport/Biloxi strip where we could met guys and dance. After we both got jobs at Gulfport High School, and really were enjoying all the coast activities and the many opportunities to meet a lot of new guys. Our weekends were nearly always full. On this particular Friday, we intended to stop off at our friends' apartment first. Betty Tynes(now Adamson) and Amy Wilkerson(now Whittenberg) and roommates nearly always had Friday night gatherings/parties at their apartment with anyone, everyone invited, but we only intended to stay long enough for me to get information about a wedding that was coming up. Then we planned to hit the strip.

Needless to say, our plans changed. As we drove up in Gloria's car and parked, we spotted two guys headed toward us. Gloria knew one of them and told me to go on up to our friends' apartment, that she was going to talk to him. So I went up. The apartment was already full, and I sat down and began talking with people. Shortly after, someone began pounding furiously on the door, then pushed the door open, came in quickly and threw his back against the door, proclaiming, "Help me! Don't let him in! He's after me!" Then everyone got quiet and waited, but nothing happened. So, everyone started talking again, mostly about that "nutty guy." Eventually, the guy, Joel, as you have probably already guessed, found a seat and started chatting with those around him. I went into the kitchen and began talking to Amy to find out future plans. That's when Betty Lou came in excited about the fellow who had just burst in. She said he was the one who had a Jaguar! I assumed she meant an animal, and everybody laughed. "No," she laughed. "A car! And not just any car! A British car! I'd give anything to get a ride in it." I knew she was nutty about fancy cars of all types and knew about all the ones in their area. She was always on the watch for unusual rides.

Pretty soon, I had all the information I needed and went to see if Gloria had come up yet. She was standing close to the front door so I went to ask her if she was ready to go. She was saying she thought she'd rather stay there, glancing at the guy she was talking with, when suddenly Joel stood up, came over to me and grabbed my left hand. "Is that an engagement ring?" he asked. "No, a birthstone," I replied. Then he took my arm and said, "Come on, I want to take you for a ride in my new car." I was shocked, like everybody around us, but he was already guiding me toward the door, and I was definitely interested in making Betty jealous about my getting a ride in a fancy car. As we started out the door and down the stairs, I said, "Hold on! I don't even know you!" So we stopped at the sidewalk and exchanged names. I asked what kind of name Siskovic was, and he answered with "Carpatho-Russian." "Are you a Communist?" I joked. He laughed and said, "Definitely not!" Then, he playfully asked,"What kind of name is Carol?" I responded, "Carol, like Christmas Carol." Then he fired right back with, "Well, I'm the First Joel! All we need between us is a little Holly!" Neither of us dreamed as we laughed together that within seven and a half years, that would be the name of our first daughter.

I did take that ride with him and learned right away that I was not allowed to push my high heels into the car carpet. I also learned that I enjoyed being with him, that he was anything but ordinary. We spent most of that night getting to know each other, and when I awoke the next morning, I heard water running in the backyard of our apartment. I looked out to find that Joel had returned the next morning and had begun washing his special car in our yard with our hose. That was the beginning of years and years of surprises of all kinds from this very special man. On our first prearranged date, he picked me up to go to my school's Friday night football game. He was wearing a suit, and he brought a book to read when he was bored with the game! Fortunately, I took a picture of him on that night, as I had brought my camera to get a picture of a school float. I keep that first picture I took of him on the wall next to the chairs where we sat side by side for so many years, where I still sit with so many good memories.

After we dated from September through December, Joel was transferred to San Angelo, Texas. I finished the school year, traveled in Europe for the summer, then started a new teaching job in Dallas, Texas, where we were reunited until he was relocated to the Philippine Islands. After a year apart, he returned to Dallas and proposed. Within a week, we were married.

Joel's prized 1963 jaguar

You Are

Part of a mountain, not the mountain itself,
but a part.
Maybe the edge that some boot knocked loose,
or a core-bit from deep within
blasted up by the vibrant forces of nature.
A force we might call God or Fate or Luck.
But here you are, my Mountain chunk,
with all your rough surfaces,
your cutting pointy angles,
your smooth and sandy sides,
your hidden parts I can't fathom.
You often act like you are the mountain,
or like you think I should think you are a mountain.
There is no way for me to say that I
like the formless piece of what you are,
love what I sense, but can never see.
"You don't ever listen," you tell me over and over.
But I do.
I hear the voice of you from long ago,
and what you are echoes what you were.
We tumble along side by side,
rubbing against each other's deformities.
Perhaps, in time, we can meld together
into one smooth solid formation of "US".

Carol M. Siskovic

Ah, The Magic

You are Kiss-a-Frog surprising!
And I suffer from no bewitchment,
no wand ever waved,
no film of mist pasted on my eyes,
From the first I knew your weirdness
your proclivity for unusual tastes,
the occasional exotic tidbit flying near,
your spontaneous unexpected leaps
from lily pad to alligator backs
to floating islands flower-bedecked.
You magical creature of green man glee.
I see no warts, no humps, no slime
Hear no burps, slurps, just rare bits.
Bug your eyes my way.
Lap me up and leap
into my waitingness,
you kissable Kermit King!

Carol M. Siskovic

Love Poem

When we are in love,
snakes, crickets and snails
make silent music
and lose their ugliness
I might even be able
to pick one up
for a pet.

Carol M. Siskovic

Our Wedding

16

In May of 1967, Joel flew from the Philippines to Dallas and arrived Sunday afternoon after having called me in the wee hours of Wednesday morning. He had said, "I'm flying there now. Will you marry me?" I'd replied, "You come, and we'll talk." We discussed all Sunday night when he arrived. I taught on Monday, and we talked again most of Monday night. We finally decided in the wee hours of Tuesday morning to go ahead, take the plunge, and get married on Saturday. I had to find a dress and a place very quickly. Our friends brought over as many borrowed wedding dresses as they could get their hands on. I also was very lucky to be able to book the chapel for 4:00 pm at the downtown Methodist Church where my roommates and I attended. The only downside was that another couple had already booked and would be getting married after us at 6:00 pm, so we had to use their decorations without disturbing them. That was perfect for us!

We would get married that Saturday so it was only a few days to plan! Engaged May 2; married May 6, 1967! Thursday evening, my roommates and I spent hours choosing a wedding dress from the many they had borrowed. The one I selected had been worn by the niece of our very good friends, Jessie Kay and Murray Hey. Murray worked for the well-known H. L. Hunt. For our two years in Dallas, they had been like parents to us, attending to our every need and taking us to dinner so often. The niece's dress was perfect, and about five years later, they told me the dress had been worn by a total of six brides. I had been number two.

At first, our parents, on hearing our news, had said there was no possible way they could make it. But on Thursday night, both called back saying they would definitely be arriving on Friday afternoon. The day before out wedding, my parents and sister drove in. Joel's mother,

Anne Pirhalla Siskovic, flew in, also on Friday. Later, on June 18, 1967, she herself would be a new bride becoming Anne Kuhar when she married Mike Kuhar. Friday night, we all had dinner together with friends at a steak house, arranged by Jessie Kay and Murray. They also arranged the reception at our apartment after the wedding.

On our wedding day, we spent all day getting ready for the wedding at 4:00 pm. The night before, however, the preacher's son with some friends had stolen hubcaps. Police had caught them and said they wouldn't charge the boys if a parent went with the sons the next day to return the hubcaps and apologize. When the preacher finished that task and finally got ready to go to the wedding at the last minute, his car keys were missing, accidentally taken by his wife. He had to call around and get someone to take him to the church. The young woman who took him was a friend of Betty Lou and Lois,' and she sat in the back of the church with shorts on. But due to the errands and missing keys, they had been 30 minutes late.

Joel and I had been apart in different sections of the church, waiting, and the organist was playing "Indian Love Call" on the organ over and over. It was 4:30, and nobody had told either of us what the delay was. Joel was alone wondering if I had backed out. So we were both really worried. My dad was so nervous by the time it started that he was shaking. I was the only child in whose wedding my father had participated. But he managed to walk me down the aisle and then to sit on the front pew beside my Mother. When the preacher asked, "Who gives this woman to be wed?" my dad stood up and firmly stated, "Her father, her mother, and God give this woman to be wed to this man." It really surprised me that he was so well spoken.

Then, the preacher started with a prayer and had me kneel on the pillow that was meant for the next bride, who had decorated the room. I was full of emotion. Joel had my next door neighbor to stand with him as Best Man. Colonel Alexander was in the Air Force and had also offered to let Joel and his Mom stay with them. My family had stayed in our apartment (a little crowded!) And my two roommates drew straws to see who would stand with me as a bridesmaid. Lois Marie

Lawson (now Naul) stood with me, and Betty Lou Tynes (now Adamson) stood with my parents.

After the wedding we went to my and my roommates' apartment for the reception. After the reception, Joel and I drove to Six Flags Over Texas at Arlington and stayed our brief honeymoon in a hotel nearby. On Sunday we had a wonderful day seeing everything in the park and riding all the rides. My parents and sister had already driven back to Mississippi, but Joel's mother called Sunday night saying she hoped to see us again before flying back. So we headed back to our apartment the next day and took her to the airport after a brief visit. On Wednesday morning, I drove Joel to Fort Worth to Carswell AF Base. He flew from there to California and and on to Guam and to the Philippines. I finished the school year, moved out, went back to my parents in Mississippi for a final visit and joined Joel in the Philippine Islands in early July, 1967.

After I had finished the school year teaching at Highland Park High School, I went home to Mississippi. I took all of my belongings to store, and I celebrated my wedding with showers among family. I prepared myself to make the long trip to the Philippine Islands to begin my marriage with Joel. Then I flew out of Memphis and stopped at Love Field in Dallas where I visited with former students Mary Webb and Beth Eldridge. Then, I continued toward California where a man boarded and sat beside me who proved very interesting and kind, and made it possible for me to spend a truly memorable evening in Honolulu at a concert with him and his wife.

Carol's Wedding Photo

THE BRIDGEPORT POST, SATURDAY

Olschwange studio

MRS. JOEL SISKOVIC

Siskovic-Malone Bridal Solemnized

Capt. Joel Siskovic Weds Miss Carol Malone in Dallas

Miss Carol Malone and Capt. Joel Siskovic were married on May 6 in the First Methodist church, Dallas, Tex., by the Rev. Harold A. Raines, Jr. The bride is the daughter of Mr. and Mrs. T. S. Malone of Minter City, Miss., and the bridegroom is the son of Mrs. Anne P. Siskovic, 273 Judson place, and the late Lt. Col. Joseph Siskovic.

The couple were attended by Miss Lois Lawson of Dallas, and Col. Wiley Alexander, also of Dallas.

The bride, a graduate of Millsaps college and the University of Mississippi, taught English at Highland Park high school in Dallas for the past two years.

The bridegroom received a degree from the University of Bridgeport. A captain in the U. S. Air Force, he is now stationed in the Philippine Islands where the couple will reside for the next year and a half.

A Sober Toast

Lift your glasses, friends.
Put them on your head,
propped just so.
We need to focus clearly,
search for neglected details.
Look close, then take them off
and fix your gaze afar.
Now close again, then far.
Close, far. Close, far.
We dwell somewhere between
the germs and mountain ranges,
ignoring both, one empowered
to cause our fall, the other to fall upon us.
Life demands three sights, at least.

So here's to our daily seeing,
and to the visions we can force
upon our eyes and minds.
Lift your glass to glasses, friends.
And drink to sober sight --
through our glasses, beyond our glasses,
and, yes, even without our glasses.

Carol M. Siskovic

17

Back in 1967, around the first of July, after Joel and I had married, I took an airplane trip to join him in the Philippine Islands. I caught the plane in Memphis and spent an overnight in Dallas. Then I flew from Dallas to Los Angeles and Los Angeles to Hawaii. In the California stop, a man came and sat in the seat beside me going to Hawaii, and we became acquainted. He was very friendly, and he found out that I had a six hour layover in Honolulu before I would fly on to the Philippine Islands to join Joel.

He asked, "What are you going to do during that six hours, just sit in the airport?" And I answered, "Yes, that's all I can do." He said, "Well, my wife is picking me up at the airport, and we're going to a special program at the University of Hawaii, and it will definitely be over by the time your plane leaves. So why don't you come and go to the program with us?" I considered but replied, "Well, I couldn't do that. I don't have a ticket." He insisted, "You don't need a ticket. Everything will work out. You just come; she's picking me up and you can see the program, and I'll make sure you get to the airport on time."

So when we landed, we went out to the front of the airport, and here came a tiny little convertible that actually wasn't his wife but a good friend of his in a two - seater convertible. He apologized and said "Well, I'm sorry, I didn't know it's would be this small, but we'll fit you in here." I propped up on the back behind the two seats somehow, so that I was way up in the air, and the wind was really blowing me. He held my arm to make sure I didn't get blown out, and we went buzzing through the streets of Honolulu and to the University of Hawaii.

We got there, and his wife was waiting outside the amphitheater for us because it was an outside program. He introduced us and said,

"Picked this girl up on the airplane, and I told her she should go to the program with us because she didn't have anything to do for the next six hours." She replied "Fine, yeah, come on. I've got a blanket thrown down on the ground right in front of the stage." So we went in and sat on the blanket, and they had brought drinks and treats. The concert started, and I hadn't even known who it was going to be. The main attraction was a girl named Buffy Sainte Marie. I remember that she sang "Listen to the Wind Blow" and "Until It's Time for You to Go." That last song has taken on special meaning for me since Joel passed, and I listen to it often since her late 1960's performance of it can be found on line. Sainte-Marie had a very trilling voice and was a fascinating performer. That Honolulu venture was the first time that I became aware of her as a noted singer.

Tommy Sands, a popular singer and actor, also performed, and then there was a performer named Josh White, who was a well known jazz performer from New Orleans. He was one of the main attractions, too. What was amazing was what had happened the previous year when my two roommates, Betty Lou Tynes and Lois Lawson, had come up to Vermont to join me after I had attended a six-week seminar on Elizabethan Arts and Literature. They had ridden the bus up to Burlington to join me, and we all rode back together in my car. We toured a lot on the way home, including New York City where we spent a few days. We were parked in a parking lot there, and as we were getting in the car to leave, I was saying, "I don't know how we get from here to the main highway to get out of New York City!" Betty looked over and said, "Here's a guy over here. I'll ask him." She went over, started talking to him and asked, "Do you live around here? Can you give us directions to get out of the center of New York and over to the highway?" He said, "I'm going that way. It's gonna go through Harlem, but I will guide you out. You just follow me, and I will take you right to the highway."

So he did. We followed him, and when we pulled over and stopped, he got out of his car, came over, and said, "Now, you just go on to that street, and you'll come right to the main highway out." We thanked him a lot, and Betty Lou asked "Where did you say you were from?" He replied, "New Orleans." She asked, "What's your name?"

and he said, “My name is Billy White.” Betty Lou was always so funny. She'd say the strangest thing sometimes. She said, “I don't guess you’re kin to Josh White. He's my favorite performer.” And he smiled and replied, “Josh White is my brother.” He was the brother of a jazz player, singer, and performer whose records we’d been playing for over a year, so we all talked for the longest time about Josh White's music. She asked, “What are you doing in New York?” and he said, "Well, I just got a job working with Revlon.” She responded, “Well, when I see Josh White next time I go to New Orleans, I'll be sure and tell him I met you.” We all laughed, and he told us goodbye and sent us on our way.

So when I was sitting there, up front at this performance at the University of Hawaii, I could not believe Josh White was being introduced. He was the last act, and he brought out his guitar and began playing and singing songs I knew well. After the show was over, the wife said, “We're going to the mayor's house on the hill. All of the performers are coming there, and we're going to have a party.” So I joined them, and I rode in the little convertible again up the winding hill to the mayor's house where I personally met Buffy Sainte Marie, Tommy Sands and Josh White. Tommy Sands seemed to be either on drugs or drink, as he sat on the floor in his t-shirt and blue jeans leaning against a wall, “out of it” most of the night.

Buffy Sainte Marie was busy with a group, and I didn't talk to her very much. But I talked to Josh White and told him I was from Mississippi. By the time they came and told me, “It's time to take you to the airport,” Josh White had learned that I was newly married, and he said, “Wait, before you go, I have to sing and dedicate a love song to you and your husband.” He got his guitar and he played a special song for me. When he finished, he put down his guitar and said, “The cost is I get a kiss from the bride.” So Josh White kissed me smack on the lips. Nobody from Mississippi would ever have believed that! He told me goodbye, and they sent me on my way to get me back to the plane. We sped down the winding streets to the airport, and I got there on time, boarded the airplane, and headed to my new husband. I never saw or heard from any of them again. I eventually learned that Josh White had died a few years later at the age of 54 during heart surgery.

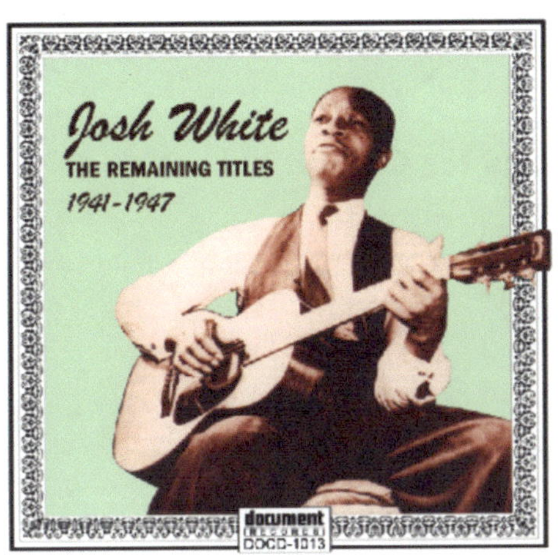
Josh White
THE REMAINING TITLES
1941-1947
document
DOCD-1013

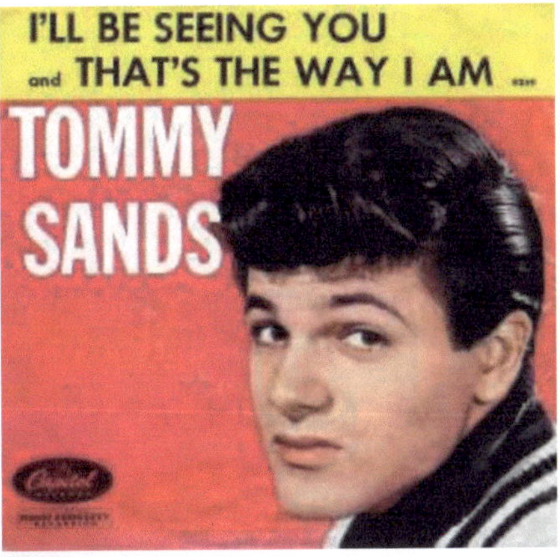
I'LL BE SEEING YOU
and THAT'S THE WAY I AM
TOMMY
SANDS

Buffy Sainte-Marie
ILLUMINATIONS

Better Than Cake and Ice Cream!

So long ago, we met by surprise,
neither of us expecting
an encounter.

In memory, our meeting, greeting,
building a sense of togetherness,
seems instantaneous.

Neither of us could then envision
years and years of sharing,
of growing — together and apart.

Of being swept up by Time,
swirled into busy lives, jobs,
everyday concerns.

Of reaching this point today when
each joyful celebration can also
bring an element of surprise:

We're still at it! And kicking! Still here!
Still feeling a special closeness to
the main treasures we possess:

Family love and lifelong friendships!

Carol M. Siskovic

18

I finally got to the Philippines and applied for a job teaching there and was hired immediately as they needed teachers. I got a job teaching seventh grade for the year, and Joel and I began our married life together there in a duplex in Balibago, just outside Clark Air Force Base. Those first few months in the Philippines, we went on numerous weekend trips and saw a lot of the territory. We had one of our best times one weekend at Pagsanjan Falls. I have a painting that celebrates that weekend and our boat trip to the Falls where Joel joined the Filipino swimmers in diving beneath the Falls and back out.

We also celebrated that night in a gathering where the Filipinos taught us how to do one of their native dances called the Tinikling in which you jump or dance between two long poles that are clapped together by two people, one at each end holding the two poles.

A month later, we went to Baguio, a mountain town called the "City of Pines" and thought of as the PI Summer Capitol. I remember a golf course there where one hole was so steep that a rotating rope had been installed to help golfers go up and down in trying to get their golf ball hit onto the green without rolling all or part way back down again. I later flew there once with a friend in a rented plane which he piloted, and we played that golf course. On the flight there, he was able to maneuver so that we got amazing views of the surrounding mountains. Joel and I also made several trips to Manilla and Subic Bay and other interesting beach areas. Then, in November, Joel left the Philippines to go to his assignment in Vietnam.

Our last day together before he left was Thanksgiving day. We went to the club at Clark Air Force Base, had our Thanksgiving lunch together, and then went to the airport. He went to Saigon, and I caught the Air Force flight that took me all the way to the Air Force Base in San Francisco. I visited with friends of Joel's there for the rest of Thanksgiving day. Then they took me to a non-military airport where I caught a plane to Memphis, Tennessee. My brother, Gwin, picked me up, and I went with his family to Mother and Daddy's house in Minter City to celebrate Thanksgiving for the third time that year. That proved to be the longest Thanksgiving day of my life. It started in the Philippines with Joel, continued with the San Francisco friends, then progressed to Tennessee, and finished in Mississippi with my parents and my brother"s family celebrating Thanksgiving together at home.

After Christmas that year, we also celebrated for a third time, and I got to be with my parents and the whole family one last time on December 28, Mother and Daddy's 43rd wedding anniversary. One of the things I kept telling myself was that Mother and Daddy were so fortunate that they had had 43 long years together. I knew that because Joel and I had been older when we married that we would probably not have 43. I didn't dream that we would have 54 years together!

Finally, the time came when I had to leave and go back to the Philippines to continue my teaching job. I prepared and packed, and I was going to take Daddy's car and drive it to Memphis to the airport. Gwin would bring the car back at his convenience. I got everything in the car, and it was so hard to tell them goodbye because I knew that Daddy was so sick. He had had surgery for lung cancer back in September. When the physician saw the state of his lungs, he just closed the surgery without removing any section. He informed the family that nothing could be done except to keep him as comfortable as possible. He also suggested that Daddy be told the operation was successful, and we should all just let him live without worry as long as possible. He said that by the time he needed to know, he would know. I was planning to come back at the end of the school year in June, and on the morning I left, I kept telling him, "I will see you in June. I'll be back." But we both knew that that might not happen, and he walked with me out the back door. At that time he was not doing a lot of walking, but he went with me out to the carport. I kissed him goodbye and hugged him, and I was struggling not to cry like crazy. I got in the car and cranked it. He took a long look at me, then stooped down as if checking my tires. The last thing I ever saw him do was check my tires.

He looked up at me and with our eyes we both said goodbye. As I backed out, it was so hard for me to leave, and I remember riding down that gravel road with tears streaming down my face. The doctor had said it was possible that he could live a year to a year and a half longer, but when I spent time with him at Christmas, I felt that he already knew his time was limited. It was just an understanding that none of us would speak. I definitely felt when he stooped down and looked at me that morning that he did not expect to see me ever again. I knew it in my heart. He died in April before I could get back to see him. I was going to Bangkok to be with Joel for my spring break when he passed, and I did not get word in time to even get back for the funeral.

Not long after I had returned to the PI to live alone in our duplex and continue teaching my seventh graders, things worsened in Vietnam, and in February, TET began, that terrible attack and massacre in Saigon. Because people were celebrating New Years and off guard in all of their activities, North Vietnamese considered it the perfect time for a surprise attach to take over all of Vietnam.

At that time, I was receiving support from a close friend stationed at Clark Air Force Base. He had grown up with me at Cagel's Crossing and was the nephew of my brother-in-law, Paul Broadway. His name was Van Higgenbotham. As soon as he learned about the TET attach, he came to tell me all he knew. He had found out that on that morning, his eighteen year old cousin Grady Muse, another of my brother-in-law's nephews had been killed. Grady had withdrawn from the University of Mississippi and volunteered in the Army. He worked in Saigon in a portable office. On the morning of TET, when he heard what he thought were firework explosions, he ran to the portable door to view them and was riddled from head to toe with gunshots. Van and I were both extremely disturbed, and he assured me that any news he got, he would relay to me. The next day or two, bodies began to arrive at Clark Air Base for transport back to the U.S. Van came to get me saying he had been given permission to escort Grady's body back home. So I drove him to the airport where we were able to watch as the planes from Vietnam unloaded bodies and reloaded them into specific planes headed for specific areas in the U.S. I watched him board with Grady's body, and that was the last time I ever saw Van. Our paths separated and we never had opportunity to meet again. My dread was that I could possibly be in that position myself as I had still not heard anything about Joel's unit. Only a few hours later, however, the commander's wife from Joel's intelligence unit got word to us that they had suffered zero casualties. It still took a long time for me to receive word from Joel personally. It was a difficult period of time for all the Clark families for the next few weeks.

Finally, the conflict lessened and Joel and I were able to communicate again and make arrangements to meet. During this time period, a good friend of mine, who lived nearby, Kathy Linton, encouraged me to join her in taking Judo lessons which were being offered on base. Over the next few months we both became fairly proficient with a number of the Judo moves. I never informed Joel of what I was doing because I wanted to surprise him with my ability when we managed to be together again. That finally happened when we were able to meet for a long weekend in Hong Kong.

I flew from Manilla, he flew from Saigon, and we met at the Hong Kong airport. We went immediately to our hotel room. When we put down all our luggage, I knew he would reach for me immediately. I had planed this moment carefully. Much to his surprise, as he reached for me, I put him in a Judo hold and threw him onto the bed! He was astonished and I could not stop laughing. "How did you do that?" he exclaimed and I told him of my long thought out, carefully conceived plan. We laughed about it for years. That weekend, we spent time with each other. After a wonderful weekend together, we caught our separate planes and parted. I flew into Manilla airport on a very rainy day, caught a taxi to the bus station to return to Clark AFB. The taxi driver was extremely kind as he took shortcuts through a drenched city and took me in a back way and then helped me load onto the bus. When I arrived at Balibago, I had to catch a Jeepney, the Philippine inexpensive jeep version of aa taxi. When he dropped me off at home, Dominique, my house keeper for me, awaited my return. One of the benefits of living in the PI at that time, was the ability to keep a full time house keeper at a minimal charge of $25 monthly. After she washed my suitcase both outside and inside, ruining the lining, Joel liked to refer to her as "Dummy" instead of Domi. I told him it was a mistake anyone could have made but it was always a joke between us.

Joel and I did not meet again until a bunch of Clark AFB people planned a Spring Vacation Trip to Bangkok, Thailand. It was during that vacation, a mixture of the best and worst feelings, that I found out that my father had died and the funeral was over. I finally received a call from Red Cross who had been trying to locate me during the last three or four days. When Joel and I parted in Bangkok, it was unforgettable. He escorted me to a US air field, got me included as a passenger in a supply support airplane. We ran across the air field to catch the plane that was already cranked and he help lift me and my suitcase into the door that was held open by an airman. I sat on a corner in a makeshift seat and arrived at Clark Air Force Base within a few hours, free of passage cost.

The next few months remained busy for both of us with a number of calls back and forth via Mars radio. I had to go on base to be able to schedule a call. Earlier on, this was also how I had talked to family form the states about my dad's illness. My school year ended, and Joel and I waited patiently for his tour to finish at the end of summer. I arranged for our household goods to be picked up and moved in with my friend Kathy for the last month of living in the Philippines.

When Joel returned, I had to say goodbye to our friends and my trusty support dog that I had unknowingly named Mestizo, which means mixed race or half breed. I had heard someone call him that and had liked the sound of that. I didn't know that it meant half breed and was a slur. By the time I did know, he had accepted it as his name. I left him with my friend and Joel and I flew back to the states. After a brief stop in Alaska and a fill week in San Francisco, we picked up his Jaguar and headed east to our new assignment at Keesler AFB in Gulfport Mississippi. There are all kinds of stories of our long trip across country but we reached Keesler, were assigned living quarters and then headed to Memphis to meet my mother and family. This was the first time for Joel to meet all of them besides Mother and Jean who had been at our wedding.

We spent the end of 1968 and the beginning of 1969 in Gulfport where I got two teaching jobs. I taught a night class for the university of Mississippi on base, and I got a full time job at Back Bay Biloxi high school teaching English. At the end of the summer, just before the arrival of a huge hurricane, we drove north to Memphis for a brief visit and the purchase of a new car before we headed to our next assignment in San Antonio, Texas.

When we moved to San Antonio, we rented a two bedroom apartment, at the Antonian Apartments on Friedrichsburg Road. Joel started his new assignment at Kelly Air Force Base and I got a teaching job at John Jay high school. Finally, we were able to settle into a somewhat normal state of married life.

Carol showing off what she learned in Judo classes with Lois while Joel watches.

Carol's 7th graders in the Philippines, June 6, 1968

Carol at a Filipino market 1967-68

Klong River Tour, Bangkok. All other pictures were stolen. Vergi and Carol with James, the tour guide, in front.

Typical Philippine Hut on stilts. Children and animals played beneath.

My dad's last healthy picture before he had cancer.

Daddy in the country store outside of Minter City.

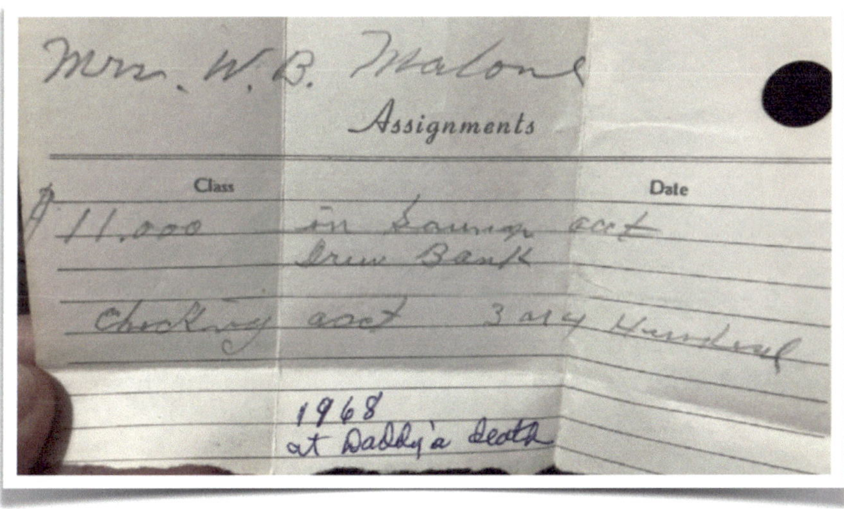

Mrs. W.B. Malone

Assignments

Class — Date

$11,000 in Savings acct
Drew Bank

Checking acct 3 or 4 Hundred

1968
at Daddy's death

He worked hard all of his life but he left his wife enough money to start a new life in Memphis in her own home down the street from her sister's house. Uncle Roy, dad's brother-in-law, helped her sell the Minter City property which gave her more money for the new house.

A Difficult Decision

My father weakly walked with me
out to the carport.
His fight with cancer had cut him in half,
withered his form, and I was leaving him
to return to my job far away
to be closer to my new best love.

Leaving him...

We hugged, kissed, cried,
talked of my return later on,
at the end of my contracted agreement.
The doctor had said don't tell him it's terminal,
when he needs to know, he will know.
Part of him knew now.

I felt the knowledge between us.
the certainty of this goodbye,
the pull that said. "Don't go."
I felt my husband's need an ocean away
and my own need for joy and a happy married life.

An ocean between.

Selfish choice won,
and guilt rode with me
all the way to the airport,
all across the sea to a place
where I could almost forget
the sight of my Daddy squatting, in pretense.

Checking my tires....

I take that picture with me everywhere,
keep it close.
A parent's last attempt to protect,
to say you go on ahead,
live life for us both.
From your first cry,
there was nothing that could not be forgiven….

Carol M. Siskovic

Children

19

During my first pregnancy in 1970, I was teaching a class of 11th graders. I had just started teaching in the mid-year, taking over for someone else who was pregnant and therefore was not allowed to continue teaching during late pregnancy. Soon after I thought I was pregnant, there was an outbreak of German Measles. Some of the students in my class really got bad cases and were very sick, so I was not sure whether that would affect my pregnancy. I went to the doctor, and they ran tests and sent them off to Washington DC, or maybe to Baltimore to one of the big hospitals, to see if my exposure had affected the baby.

It took a long time, and so it was months before I knew for sure that the pregnancy did not seem to have been affected. What a relief! The rest of the pregnancy went pretty smoothly, and then on the evening of December 2, I started to feel some occasional pains. It was the first pregnancy so I didn't quite know what it was, but when I woke up in the early morning. I called Wilford Hall and said, "I may be having labor pains. I don't know. Should I come in?" The nurse said, "Yes, you can come in." What I didn't find out until later was that she should have said, "Come in immediately." She didn't use that word so I thought that I had plenty of time to get there. No hurry at all.

I woke Joel, and we took our time getting dressed and getting everything together. We were so excited, but decided that we would go have breakfast first. We went to our usual Waffle House just down the street. By this time it was almost 7 o'clock, and we sat down at the booth where we could look out the window and watch the day dawning. At that time, they had small juke boxes at your table where you could put a quarter in and play some songs. We chose "We've Only Just Begun" by the Carpenters. I think we played it about three times and ate our waffles and smiled and smiled at each other. We gazed across Fredericksburg Road in San Antonio which at that time didn't have any buildings, and you could see far off toward the city. We thought about our future and what was the beginning of our family on that day. Finally, we finished, and we got in the car and headed toward Wilford Hall, and I still wasn't having a lot of labor pains.

But as we progressed toward Wilford Hall, they started coming. They were increasing a little bit more often and then a little bit harder, and when we pulled into the Wilford Hall parking lot, we pulled up close to the front and got out of the car. Joel was getting my suitcase out of the backseat, and I went around to the back of the car and propped myself on the car because all of a sudden I felt something happening inside my body. I didn't know what it was.

I'm standing there leaning on the car, and suddenly, water came pouring, gushing, out of me. I said "Joel…" I had heard of the water breaking, but I didn't realize that you wouldn't be able to control it at all. The water was just pouring and running down the street. When he came around the end of the car, he saw it. I said, "I think my water broke." He suddenly opened the front door, jumped in the driver's seat, and just sat there with his head in his hands and waited for it to be over. I started laughing, and as I laughed, the harder the water poured, and the farther it went down the street. Joel was so embarrassed, and I kept laughing and laughing. Finally, it stopped and he got out and said, "I think we can go in now…" so we entered and checked in.

We went up to the third-floor, and I was telling everybody the story, which started a whole day's worth of funny hospital birthing stories. They assigned me a room because they didn't think anything was going to happen that soon. They said it could be a long time, and they turned to Joel, knowing he didn't know what to do with himself, and said, "You probably should just go on to work and tell them your wife is in the hospital. When it gets close, we'll give you a call, and you'll be here in plenty of time." He said "OK," and he left. The rest of the morning became a huge joke. They started laughing about the water-breaking story and telling all kinds of other funny things that had happened. It became a day of storytelling, Everybody had a favorite, including the little nurse who had been trapped under a rather large woman who had fainted and fallen on her as she had tried to catch her.

At noon, a doctor came in and he said, "Your friend is my neighbor. She called me and said you were up here and that I should take your case." He took care of me the rest of the day, starting immediately. He said, "We're going to stop all this guessing," because the nurses had started writing on my stomach their guesses as to whether it was a boy or girl and how many pounds they thought it would weigh. I already had writing all over my lower abdomen. He said, "I'm taking you down, and we're gonna get an x-ray, and I will tell you exactly what it is."

Before we went for the x-ray, he said, "This baby is a boy. I'm never wrong. I listen to the heartbeat, and I can tell this baby is a boy and is going to weight about 7 pounds. It turned out later that he was right. He did the x-rays by one o'clock, and at that time he said, "We've been fooling around all day, and your readiness for delivery is not changing at all. I'm gonna give you something so you can start the labor slowly." They gave me medicine and the labor began, but it was very slow. Joel finished at work and came back, and we still had a long time to wait. I did not deliver until almost midnight. The birth finally occurred just three minutes before midnight. I had been hoping that the baby would be born before midnight because I knew that December 3 was my Daddy's older sister's birthday. I thought it would be so nice if my first baby was born on Aunt Curt's birthday because she had given me special attention as a baby and had crocheted a complete baby outfit for me. She also had helped name me. Nobody ever told me whether Frances or Carol was her choice, but I knew she had given me one of my names and Daddy had picked the other one.

I finally went into the delivery room, and at that time the fathers did not go into the delivery room. Most fathers didn't want to go. But Joel wanted to be there, and he was probably the first at Wilford Hall Hospital to attend and record on audio tape the entire delivery. He took his tape recorder in, so we have, saved for posterity, our first words and everything that was said during our son's delivery. When the baby came out and the doctor held him up, it was interesting that the baby had bright red hair. It was so obvious, and a lot of bright red hair. The doctor was holding him up right in front of him, and I looked at my baby, and I looked at the doctor, and their hair was the exact same color. Joel blurted, "Carol, does the baby have red hair?" and we all started laughing again. "Where did that red hair come from?" We spent the next few weeks with family arguing about whose side the red hair came from. We determined finally that we both had some red hair in our families. My Mother's Mother, now gray, had had some red in her hair, and Joel's mother said that one of their relatives had had red hair also. So both sides of the family got to take credit for Lee's red hair. We named him Joel Elias Siskovic, II, and we decided to call him Lee, which was short for Elias, Joel's maternal grandfather's name in Carpatho-Russian. We thought Lee would be a good nickname to distinguish him from his father, and we decided on it at the beginning of December 4. We both went sound asleep that night, so happy with a very healthy first child. Before sleeping, Joel had had a good time waking people up with the news.

In 1972, I gave birth to my second baby, and this one was born in March of the year. My mother had come to visit and help. Lee was walking at that time, and we went to the San Antonio airport to meet her. She had flown into Dallas with my sister-in-law, Wendy, because she had never flown before. That was her first airplane flight, and she was scared to go alone. Wendy got off to visit her sister in Dallas, and Mother came the rest of the way alone. Lee and I went to the airport and were waiting for the plane to land. Those were the days when you could go right up to the entrance where the passengers exited from the plane. Lee was so cute, and when I saw her coming through the doorway, I said, "There's Mamalone, go hug her." Smiling, he went toddling up to her. She couldn't believe it when he grabbed her around the knees and hugged her. After we got her luggage, got in the car, and went home, he was so happy to have somebody special to give him attention. She made banana pudding, a favorite of mine, that evening because she could make them so fast and so good. Later, around 9 pm, I started having some labor pains, and I thought, "I'm not gonna get any more of that banana pudding if I don't eat it tonight." So I ate banana pudding like crazy.

I didn't tell that I was having labor pains, but I think Mother suspected it because I went in and took a long bath, and I had my suitcase all packed and was looking around into everything. I was giving her instructions on what to do, and she asked, "Are you going into labor?" Finally, I said, "Yes, but I don't think I have to go until tomorrow morning." I woke up, however, about 4 o'clock, and I thought "Yeah, I think I better go now!" I woke Joel up, and we got ready. Then I woke Mother, and told her, "I'm going in now. It's working a little faster than the other one." She replied, "Well, usually the more babies you have, the faster the labor comes on." And she was right. On the way, I really started having labor pains very fast, and we barely made it in time. We got into Wilford Hall, and my water had not broken yet, but I still was having very strong labor pains. As soon as we got there, they said, "Oh yeah, you're in big labor. We're just gonna go ahead and break your water." We'd arrived there just a little before seven, and Holly was born at 7:20 in the morning. And it was a wonderful birth! It was a very healthy girl! Everything went very smoothly, and Joel left us and allowed me to get some rest. He went back to get Mother, and they returned together to see the new baby. When I had seen my baby, my first thought was, "Oh, that poor baby! She's all scrunched up, and she's going to be so ugly." I was so worried that Holly was not going to be a pretty girl! I don't know why that bothered me, but when Mother came in, I immediately cried, "Oh, Mother, her face is just all scrunched up and everything. It's just terrible. I don't know how she's going to live like that." And she replied, "Nonsense! That's the most beautiful baby I have ever seen in my life!" One thing I knew about my mother was that she never lied, and she sure wasn't ever going to lie to make anybody feel better. As soon as she said that, I thought, "Oh, it must be okay." Pretty soon, they brought the baby to me, and I realized that when I had first seen her she had not yet recovered from the birthing process. My mother was right! She was just beautiful, just gorgeous, and I was so happy. That was on a Thursday morning. They usually kept you in the hospital for three days, but early on Sunday morning, also Easter Sunday, we were able to go home early. Joel had been with me for her birth, also, and had recorded it, too.

We started home that Sunday morning, but I felt so good, and it was Easter Sunday. So we decided that we would stop at Luby's Cafeteria and have our Easter dinner because neither one of us wanted to cook. So we took our new baby in, went through the line choosing our food, then set the baby seat right on our table, watching her as we ate our Easter meal together. She was sleeping so blissfully, and everybody came by and said, "This baby looks like it was just born!"

She was only three days old! People couldn't believe it. We hadn't even thought about the fact that it might not be good for a newborn baby to be out in public, but she did just fine. Of course, Lee was so proud of his little sister, and we were a very happy family on that Easter day!

On the night that Joel and I had met eight years previous, we had had an interesting verbal exchange. I was Christmas Carol and he was the First Joel! All we needed together was a little Holly!" That interchange remained in our minds, and we knew that we would name our girl baby Holly. When she was born, it only seemed fitting to also name her Bianca in honor of her grandmother Blanche, her grandmother Anne, and her Mother Carol. Holly Bianca Siskovic, our first born daughter.

When Holly was only three months old, Joel was transferred to Fort Meade, Maryland, just outside DC. We purchased our first home in Bowie, Maryland, and lived there until 1975 when we were transferred to England. Our third child was born while we lived in Bowie, Maryland, and because it was my third baby, I wasn't worried much at all. I thought it was pretty much "old hat" for me now. I had arranged with two teenagers who lived a few houses down the street to come whenever I went into labor and to babysit Lee and Holly. I didn't think that it would begin in the middle of the night. I went to bed early on the 27th of October, thinking that everything was okay. But as the night progressed, I began to have labor pains that grew more and more and more. Finally, at about 3:30 or 4:00, I realized "I'm not going to make it until daylight" so I woke Joel. I told him, "I think you better go down the street and get the girls and bring them down here because we're not going to have much time before we have to go to the hospital."

Bowie, Maryland, was maybe 12-15 miles from the Annapolis Naval Base Hospital. We had been using the Navy Base for our medical needs so I had planned to go there to deliver the baby. I didn't think it would take long to get the sitters and then get to the hospital. So Joel went down the street and got the girls, two sisters who were going to take turns. One of them came, and she said her sister would be joining. Then we got everything together and made the trip. It was still dark when we arrived at the hospital, but I hadn't realized that the hospital was going to be so much different from Wilford Hall in San Antonio where I had delivered Lee and Holly.

This was a hospital devoted largely to young male sailors, and there were very few women in there. They had a delivery department so I went in, and it was like "hooray!" They were so glad to have a patient that they could give their attention to. So I received the best care in the world, and they did everything for me that was possible. The delivery was slow, but uneventful for the most part. Cara was my largest baby born of our four, so it took a little longer for her to deliver, and I had to push a little harder, but there was no problem with her birth at all. We had decided that if this one was a girl, we would name her after ourselves, Carol Jo, and call her Cara. As soon as she was born, they wheeled me out to the hall and put us in front of a huge plate glass window that looked into the nursery. The nurse came with the baby who was in a blanket, all curled up, in a tight little bundle. Then the nurse placed her on top of a tall counter with a pad on it, right in front of the window. She undid the blanket for us to see, and we watched Cara slowly stretch herself out. I kept saying, "Look at that! Look, look, look, look at that." She stretched longer and longer, and Joel knocked on the glass. He said, "How long is the baby?" The nurse started laughing, and she reached over for a tape measure and started measuring how tall Cara was. As she had stretched out, it seemed like she was over two feet long. We laughed and laughed, and we were so proud and happy. She was perfectly healthy, and so beautiful, and nobody could've ask for a better birth. we would never have guessed she would turn out the shortest of our children. I was wheeled immediately to my room and provided with chocolate cake and a meal, and I was taken care of like I was the queen of Sheba for the rest of my stay there.

It was about that time that Joel came home one afternoon with a great buy that he had come across and absolutely could not bypass. It was a 1970 Volkswagon camper van, complete with sliding door, bed, small fridge, and sink. With three children now, it made sense, he said, to have a second vehicle and especially one that made long drives with kids a lot easier. Plus, we could camp on long trips, avoiding motel fees. We just needed a little more sleeping room, which he soon solved by having a pop-top installed, complete with another bed. It was shortly after the installation of the pop-top on the VW camper that Joel decided that it now suited us perfectly as a family. The top reminded him of a turtle shell, and we as a family might be slow, usually were, but we "got there just the same" and often " even won the race!" Now, he proclaimed, it could truly be said, "We carry our homes on our back." We, too, were TURTLES! And we have remained "Turtles" to this day!

When Cara was about a year and a half, we received orders to move from Bowie, Maryland, to Chicksands Air Force Base in England. So in 1975 we prepared for the move and headed out with our new baby to spend the next four years living in England.

Then early in 1977, I realized that I might be pregnant again. Joel's stepfather had passed away, and we had to return with the children to Connecticut for his funeral. After the funeral, my mother flew from Memphis, Tennessee, to visit with us for a few days before we headed back to England. One day, in the kitchen, Joel's mother and my mother were talking. They said, "Joel and Carol have such a lovely family." Joel's mother said, "I think their family is complete. Don't you, Blanche?" My mother looked at her and said, "Well, yes, I guess so." By that time I was pretty certain I was pregnant, but I just smiled and said nothing.

As soon as we got back to England, I verified for certain that I was pregnant. But I still didn't say anything for a while because I thought, "Well, this will be my last pregnancy, and it will be my little secret for a bit." So I didn't even tell Joel. Very soon, though, we went to a big dance on a Friday night, and I had on what I thought to be an unrevealing dress. Toward the end of the dance and the party, the Colonel's wife came over to Joel and said, "Joel, I'm so happy for you and Carol." And he asked, "What do you mean?" She replied, "Well, she's obviously pregnant…" and Joel said, "You have to tell her then." We left right away, and in the car he hesitantly said, "You won't believe what the Colonel's wife said to me." As he began to tell me, I starting laughing, and he exclaimed, "You are pregnant!" And I beamed, "Yes, WE are pregnant."

So that was the beginning of Jeannie's pregnancy. Our last child, Jean Elizabeth. We decided to name her after my sister, Jean, and the Queen of England. I also had a very good friend I'd known since high school and keep in touch with to the present day whose name was Elizabeth. So I always said she was named after the queen, and after my friend, but especially after my sister. Also my grandmother, my Dad's mother, Elizabeth Jane Malone, we'd be honoring by naming her Elizabeth. I don't think any other grands or great grands were ever named Elizabeth. Jean Elizabeth was our fourth child. We decided to call her Jean E. or Jeannie. I was a "fourth child," and I always said a fourth child will always be "trouble." So it seemed that Jeannie and I both decided that we would always go our own way and do whatever we deemed best. I think Jeannie would probably agree with me that we are both truly independent souls!

When Jeannie was born, I knew early on in the wee hours of Saturday morning that I was getting ready to deliver. A very good and dear friend, Ruth Brazier, worked for me as a housekeeper and nanny, and I had already arranged with her that she and her husband, Jim, would come and keep the three children while Joel and I went for Jeannie's delivery to RAF Lakenheath. On that Saturday morning, I woke Joel and said, "Today is the day. You need to call Ruth and tell her and her husband to prepare to come and get the kids." He did, and I just told him to tell her there was no hurry. Things were going very slowly so they came in and got there about 10 o'clock in the morning. They took the kids as they were going to take them to their house to stay for the duration of the birth. Among their many activities while we were gone, they ended up painting rocks for us during that time, and I still have them to this day.

Joel and I left the kids in Ruth's care, and we got in our VW van and started for Lakenheath, which would take about two hours to reach. As soon as we hit the road, I began to realize an increase in labor intensity. So I told Joel that we had to pull over. I was going to pull out the bed so that I could lie down for the trip. It was a good thing I did because the longer we went, the harder the labor became, and the faster the labor pains. I didn't think my labor would increase that quickly. We came to a little town pretty close to Lakenheath. It was Saturday, and that was market day in that town and cars were lined up. We came to a complete stop right in front of a fire station. Joel said, "Oh, I'm just gonna run in real quick and see if anybody in the fire station can deliver." I said "okay" so he just left the car running and ran in. They said emphatically, "No! We don't do deliveries. We don't deliver babies. You need to head for a hospital." He came back to the VW, and all of a sudden he heard a pecking on the window. Next-door neighbors from Chicksands Air Force Base had been behind us and said, "You may not know it, but we are right behind you. Do you need any help?" Joel, relieved, replied, "Just stick with us! We don't know what's going to happen. We're trying to make it to the hospital before she delivers."

They stuck right with us, and it took longer than we expected. But, finally, the traffic began to move. We drove as quickly as we could and pulled into Lakenheath just after 2pm. As soon as we pulled into the delivery area, Joel jumped out of the car, left me, didn't say anything. He went running inside and then came back. I started trying to get up on my own and get out. But by the time I got the sliding door open, they were there with a wheelchair and they got me out, put me in the chair, raced me into the building, onto the elevator, up to the second or third floor, across to the delivery room, and they said, "You're lucky! The doctor is already in the delivery room. He just delivered a baby." They pushed me in there and right onto the delivery table.

The whole process of delivery wasn't long at all. It was 20-30 minutes at the most until Jeannie was born. I pushed when she was born. I was struggling, struggling, and then she came out! The doctor said, "And here she is!" That was the first time we found out that it was another girl. A third girl! We waited, and we waited…. Everything was so quiet…so quiet. The doctor cut the cord and gave her to nurse. Still not a sound. Not a sound.

Two nurses went over to the side, and Joel and I were holding our breath. Everything was so still, and the doctor went over to the side. Nothing. Nothing. Nothing. We couldn't breathe. We didn't know what had happened, and nobody was making any noise. Then, all of a sudden, the most beautiful sound in the world began. The beginning cries of a newborn baby! Everybody breathed deeply and in unison said "Oh…." And I started laughing. I mouthed, "She's fine!" She was screaming to her heart's content, and it was so good! She was still a little blue when I got her. My first sight of her was a blue, blue, baby. But she recovered quickly, and they brought her to me. I told the doctor, "Well, this is our last child, and I hope you're ready to make sure that will be the case." He said, "I'll check and make sure that we can take care of that." And the next day he did. Our family was complete.

We lived in England for the next two years and had many other adventures together. We did a good deal of traveling during that time. Joel and I traveled all over England and Ireland and Scotland. We even went to Paris, France, and we took one last trip early in 1979 to Israel. It was probably the best tour that we ever went on. It was wonderful, and the fortunate thing during that whole time was that I had Ruth Brasier to be like a grandmother, a big sister, a good friend, and a babysitter for me. All the kids loved her dearly. As did Joel and I. She even came to visit us after we returned to the States.

Those years in England were so enjoyable, but in 1979, we finally had to move. Joel had chosen San Antonio, Texas, to be his last station before retirement. We had lived there earlier in our marriage. Lee and Holly had been born in San Antonio, and we thought that it would be a place where we would really like to settle. We didn't get to San Antonio immediately; we had a brief vacation and went to Connecticut to spend some time there. Then we drove slowly down to Memphis, Tennessee, and visited with all the Memphis relatives, and then the Mississippi relatives. We traveled in a 1969 Mercury Cougar that had been bought the year before Lee was born. One of his earliest pictures was him as a toddler trying to get a key into the Mercury door. So we made sure that he inherited that car, and he has it to this day.

We rented a trailer and attached it to the cougar to make the long trip. We had shipped the VW van to New Orleans to be picked up, so we drove both vehicles from New Orleans. Joel and I split up, and one of us would drive one car and one the other all the way from New Orleans into San Antonio. We stopped at 2 AM at a motel in San Antonio and stayed there. Then we checked in at the Kelly Field Air Force Base and began the process of searching for a permanent house. It took several weeks, but we eventually bought the house at 6401 Cairo in San Antonio, Texas 78229, and have lived here in this house ever since. From 1979 to the present day. The kids were all small when we began our time as a family in San Antonio in 1979. Then, in 1980, I began teaching at John Jay High School. I taught there for 18 years and at Communications Arts School for the next 7 years, all the way through until 2005 when I retired. During that time, I also taught night classes for San Antonio Jr. College, Palo Alto Jr. College, Northwest Jr. College, and UTSA(University of Texas at San Antonio).

My kids always had love, and books, and siblings, and friends. Every summer we drove to Mississippi to have family reunions, and they got to know my extended family. We didn't spoil the kids, but we made sure they had so many things that we wanted growing up. They all had after-school sports or piano or dance lessons. They all finished high school knowing they would go to college. They all knew they could be anything they put their minds to become. Each of them finished college and got their masters degrees or more. Holly got her Masters Degree in Instructional Technology and taught kindergarten. Cara got her doctorate degree in Education, taught, and then became "right-hand" for several business entities. Lee passed the bar and became an agent, then a lawyer for the FBI. Jeannie learned several languages and worked internationally and became a government worker, then a Vice President for a company. Generations of sacrifices, hard work, and determination, plus care and consideration for others, seemed to settle in these children. They were and are their parents' greatest pride and joy!

A table juke box

The song we listened to before
Lee was born

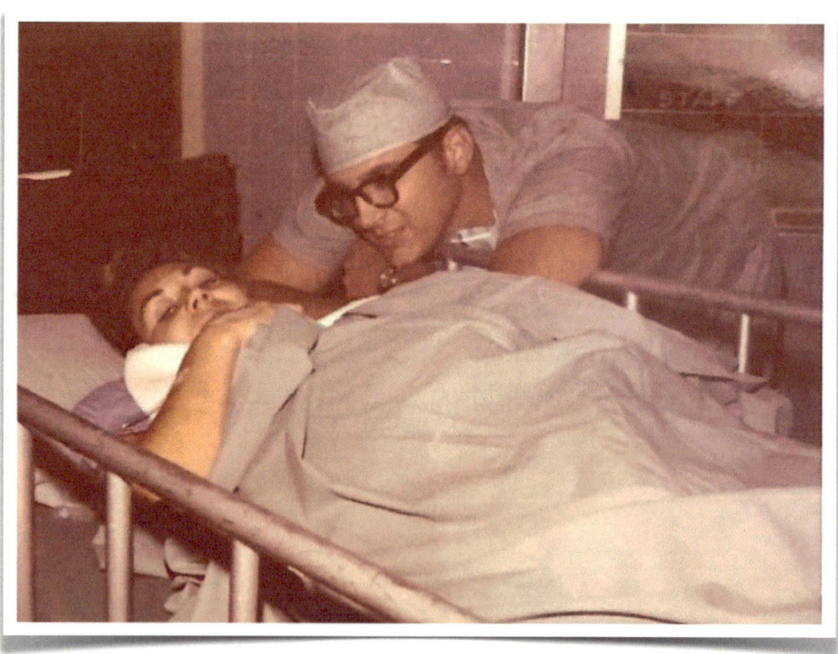

Joel in scrubs for the delivery room

The Winds!

Stillness can bring peace,
even comfort, a coating of joy.
But, eventually, we cease
to need the wrap of sameness.

We watch the sky for a sign
of approaching change,
a breezy hint of hope to realign,
allay our dreary oppression.

We desire a w h i r l i n g, STRONG wind
to lift move change relieve <<< .
Swift, but not too dangerous - enough to bend~nd~nd
us, make us better, without breaking.

Enough to disseminate sultriness, bring gifts
of nurture and sweet green hope
that rejuvenate and once again lift
our sagging spirits, send us forth to cope.

Blow, wind, blow!
Bring on the rain!
Renew all that we know!
Whip and wash away the pain!

Carol M. Siskovic

Total Distraction

A squirrel sneaked in,
scampering, rustling my brain.
It's making a home.

Carol M. Siskovic
(Woke at 7AM with this Haiku as a gift)

Dubious Willingness

Babies, just born, often scream.
Squeezed or pulled into bright light,
into openness unchosen.
Obvious distress and unwillingness
voiced before a temporary calming.
Hands, hands, touching, moving,
mostly unwanted at first.
All that follows is a slow progression
in search of whatever soothes, pleases.
The doubt always hovers, hidden by
hopeful smiles, reaching arms,
eyes peering for something, someone,
to fulfill what feels like a promise.
Like a cliff's edge, no landing in sight.

Parents beam, brag, oohing, aahing.
Squelching their own creeping doubts,
remembered fears, vast uncertainties.
Here lies a little self, or copy of self,
totally dependent on forces undefined,
on old commitments made silently
generations ago by cells evolving,
producing and producing, multiplying
without benefit of guarantee or warranty.
Accidental collision of universal bits
suddenly blessed somehow with a strange
circle of radiating protectiveness and need.
No revelation of why, how. Together,
the only answer. And the smiles continue.

Carol M. Siskovic

20

In 1979 our tour in England was finished, and our next assignment was to San Antonio, Texas. Joel knew it was to be his final tour before retirement so he selected San Antonio as the final place, knowing that we wanted to find our final home for the next part of our lives. We thought that Texas might prove a good choice, particularly San Antonio, so when we came, we went house-searching with the idea that it would probably prove our final location. We found a really good agent, and for a week, maybe eight or 10 days, she showed us homes all over the San Antonio area, which covered far less territory 45 years ago. I'm not sure how exactly, but we finally decided on our house at 6401 Cairo Drive, and we have lived there ever since.

This is my house alone at the present time, but all our children grew up in this house on Cairo Drive and still think of it as home. The night we completed the paper work, the agent brought us all to the empty house, and while the adults drank toasts with wine the agent had provided, the children ran all about the empty house, choosing their rooms and enjoying the spaciousness before the furniture would arrive. On September 25, our furniture and belongings arrived. Joel planned the placement, and many of the pieces have not been moved since then because he had laid it out so perfectly. The movers themselves were amazed that he was able to measure the space needed, then set all the pieces up out on the front lawn. To their surprise, everything fitted and looked perfect when they moved them inside and placed them exactly as he had set them up. For forty-five years, they have remained in place just as they were arranged that day. Most of the pieces are beautiful wood made to order and purchased in England. They weighed so much that Joel had to give up the purchase of a very desirable red phone booth which would have made us very overweight. He always regretted that loss as he had a huge collection of old phones, and that booth would have really capped it off.

After we had lived here about a year, since the children were all in school and daycare, we decided that I could probably do some substituting. Lee was in fourth grade, and Holly was a second grader, both just down the street at Glenoaks Elementary School. Cara was in kindergarten at Trinity Methodist, and Jeannie was in daycare at Shepherd of the Hills Lutheran Church. I decided that I could do some shopping around for teacher substitute work, so I contacted Northside School District where I had formerly worked to tell them I would like to activate my record and start doing some subbing. About an hour or two later, I got a call back. My record was activated, but they were in need of a permanent English teacher at John Jay High School where I had taught 10 years ago, and they wondered if I would be interested in applying for that job. I said I hadn't really planned to start teaching full-time yet, but I would think about it and call back within an hour. I called Joel, and we talked.

He said, "Well, you know I'm retiring soon, and it would be really good if you had a job. We would have some additional income until I decide what works for me as a next career." He said there was really no reason why I couldn't quit if it didn't work out. So I called back and agreed to go for an interview that afternoon, like two hours later. I dressed quickly, went in for the interview, and met Roger Harris, principal, and Nelda Andrewartha, English Department head. Nelda was obviously so embarrassed because she had been working in her room in blue jeans and sweaty t-shirt , totally unprepared to do an interview. They must have been pretty desperate because they hired me immediately to teach ninth and tenth grade English classes. So, after a ten-year interim, I returned to teaching that August of 1980. I then taught at John Jay for a total of 18 more years. I finally left Jay after receiving an opportunity to teach in a newly established school in the district, Communication Arts High School, a specialty school attached to Taft High School. I would be teaching their first senior class, and that seemed like a good opportunity for me, so I accepted that job in 1998 and stayed there until I retired in 2005. It turned out to be a perfect transition for my last seven years of teaching.

Shortly before I retired, I was named Teacher of the Year for the Northside School District and then English Teacher of the Year for Texas Council of Teachers of English. Both of those honors were much appreciated and capped off my teaching career. I had thought when I retired that I would continue teaching part-time classes as I had for years at San Antonio Community College, Northwest Vista Community College, Palo Alto Community College, and UTSA (University of Texas at San Antonio). I had thought I would continue teaching night classes or maybe even move to some daytime classes. Instead of having to go in every day, I would only commit to maybe an hour a day, once or twice a week - whatever worked out.

But as it turned out, our children married, moved to different places, began their own families. We found we wanted the freedom to travel and visit them whenever we felt the urge, so I never took another job that would keep me confined to San Antonio. Instead, Joel and I began our traveling and RVing years. Jeannie was living in the DC area, Cara was either in DC, South Carolina, or North Carolina, and Lee lived in Memphis, Tennessee, or in Pennsylvania. We went to see them all, and we both had relatives from Mississippi to New York and Connecticut. Plus, there were just places we wanted to go and see. Holly's family was the only one in San Antonio.

When we started our retirement in 2005, we didn't have any grandchildren, but in 2006 the first grandchild was born. The last one was born in 2020. During all of these years, we wanted to be available to visit our children, or to receive our children as visitors whenever they could come, so neither of us ever returned to teaching or to any other job commitment. I had been a teacher for thirty-three years total. Joel had spent twenty years in the Air Force, then worked for a retired general for almost a year before taking a job with a company called ISN which dealt in intelligence work and high security contracts. After working at ISN from 1984 to 1998, he took a job as Technology Director for Edgewood Independent School District until 2005. That was the year we both retired and began our years of freedom together.

We spent our time following our hobbies and following our hearts, doing whatever we felt we wanted to do. Those were really enjoyable years during our sixteen years of retirement together. Joel's health, however, was slowly declining. It became worse and worse because of his PTSD and several exposures that he had endured while in Vietnam. By this time he had learned that he was diabetic and had some lung problems. Slowly slowly, he began to have more and more breathing problems so that he had to have a CPAP machine, and then finally went onto full-time oxygen. He became less able to move around. Then his eyesight failed, and he was unable to drive, so I became the full-time driver. Very slowly, we moved into our retirement existence, which always seem to stay busy. We always had plenty to do, and when we didn't, we enjoyed just being together, doing whatever we felt like at the moment. We had a very, very pleasurable time as partners in life, but as he got more disabled, I had to take more responsibility for everything as he was able to do less and less. First, he was on oxygen full-time. Then he went to a scooter full-time. He was unable to walk around more than a step or two, and we spent much of our time at the VA hospital and in the medical center going to various doctors for various reasons. So we devoted ourselves to extending our life together as long as we possibly could.

When Joel died, our children came together, and each contributing in a special way, they put together a perfect celebration of their father's life which occurred on August 14, 2021, the day after what would have been his 81st birthday. Though now passed on, he has never left our thoughts, our hearts, our memories. In the many framed pictures the children have placed around the house, he smiles on us and watches. And we always feel his undying love.

Somewhere Right Now

A baby is exiting the tight soft dark
and whirling through the long interval
before the lungs awake to outside air,
before the eyes blink to a new blur
and just before the first grip of human hands.

Across the way an old body rasps one last
lovely memory into the close circle of watchers
and they breathe into themselves something
of all that had been before the crumbling.
The wrinkles, the feebleness and the white pain
jump upon a silent laugh and ride away
right now.

And between these two mysteries millions walk
unaware, heedless of synchronicity,
of simultaneous meteors streaking and burning
like sparks from some eternal fire
that roars and roars and roars,
but will not ever be consumed.

Carol M. Siskovic

21

As a child I had never written a poem. In fact, I had no knowledge of poetry at all, I guess, until I received a book gift from Granny Cagle that was full of children's nursery rhymes. From those I got some idea of rhythm and rhyme, but I really hadn't received much training. In eighth grade, after I started to Clarksdale Jr. High, I began to be introduced to pieces of literature that would be considered true poetry. I hadn't had much experience reading poems until in the eighth grade. Miss Persons, my English teacher, gave us an assignment on one March Friday. We were going to go into a poetry unit the following week so at the end of class, she said, "I want everyone of you to write a poem over the weekend and turn it in Monday morning." I went home, terrified, not knowing what a poem was or how in the world I would begin to write one. That Saturday morning, my dad, as he did every morning, went out to feed the hogs and the cows and do his farm work, and afterwards, he came onto the back porch stomping his feet and clapping his hands. He exclaimed loudly, "It's cold again! It's Blueberry Winter! As soon as I heard that expression, though I had no idea what Blueberry Winter was, I thought that could be the title of my poem. So I got him to explain that it was a sudden unexpected, even refreshing, cold spell after Winter was supposedly past. And it was refreshing, in more ways than one. Inspired, I somehow wrote my first poem. I even entitled the poem "Blueberry Winter" when I completed it, though that might not have been the most creative choice. I could hardly wait to get it in final form and turn it in Monday morning.

After we reported to class, and she started her poetry unit, Miss Persons didn't mention our poems again all period. I wanted so much to read mine to somebody and to get some reaction, but at the end of the class she said, "OK, now take out your poems that you wrote and pass them up." They were collected, the bell rang, and we were dismissed. I waited patiently days and days to get some report on the poems, or for us to share in some way. When, finally, we finished the poetry unit, and I had almost forgotten about sharing, she brought out a folder, and she had a student in the class hand back all the poems. When they were all given out, she chose one boy to read and nobody else, so I didn't even get to read my poem to the class. Of course, I wanted to see what she had written about the poem. At the top of the page on mine, she had written "Good job!" Nothing else! Not a mark on it! Nothing! I looked at other people around me. They had the same exclamation and no comments. I did get an A! I didn't know if everybody got an A, but that was the only response to my poem that I ever received. The poem went into my files, then on through high school, college and years of marriage in a folder in my school and traveling trunk. That trunk, after trips to college, Yellowstone, Gulfport, Dallas, Maryland, and England, suddenly disappeared during our move from England back to San Antonio in 1979. I had no other copies, so my first poem has disappeared forever as I remember nothing of it except the title.

It was years after that first poem before I eventually developed a real interest in poetry. I didn't write any more poetry in high school, but I began to read a lot of poetry and study a lot in my upper classes and when I went to college. I eventually began to try to write a few poems, and by the time I was teaching, I was feeling a little more daring in writing more poems. My roommate the first few years of teaching, Gloria Sultan, took an interest in my poetry and was probably the most encouraging person I had ever come across. She praised and motivated me to try more, and I continued writing from that point on. Because of my own experiences, I always tried to encourage my students, and I gave them comments as soon as I could whenever they gave me a poem or whatever they shared with me. There were a lot of them who felt exactly as I had, afraid to share, afraid they were no good, that their poems didn't make sense and had no “poetic” beauty. I knew that before they could write freely that I had to help them overcome their fears and build the courage to share. Only then would they be able to express themselves, knowing that responses would be as various as the people who responded, that the real joy came in the creating, the capturing of the poetic gift of words, the saving and the savoring. If anyone else enjoyed or gained from the poem, that would simply be additional happiness, not expected or necessary.

I taught a total of thirty-three years, the first two at Clarksdale Middle School, teaching eighth grade English in the same building where I had been taught eighth grade English by the very stern Miss Persons. One day early in my first teaching year, the class became very still and I became aware that a person was standing at my classroom door, just observing. When I approached to ask if I could help, I suddenly recognized her as an aged Miss Persons, whom I had apparently replaced, nine years after I had first walked into her classroom as a student. She looked me over, hard, then said, “I am moving and I just wanted to come by one last time to tell you this one thing: “Love’em…but be HARD AS NAILS!” Then, not waiting for any kind of response, she turned and walked away. I don’t know for certain, but I believe it was good that I chose to follow only the first part of that advice.

After the second year at Clarksdale, my roommate ole, Gloria, and I made the choice to seek jobs at Gulfport, Mississippi, where we taught for two years. I taught eleventh grade English the first year, then added journalism and publications the second year, responsible for the printing of the yearbook and the monthly school newspaper. That was definitely my favorite class to teach up to that point, and it was only replaced by Creative Writing years later which also included the publication of a creative writing collection named PARNASSUS. After two years at Gulfport, I took a job in Dallas, Texas, at Highland Park High School, where I taught junior and senior English and remained for two years before getting married and moving to the Philippine Islands where I taught seventh grade English for a year at Clark Air Force Base. After we left the PI, we were located for a year at Kessler AFB in Biloxi, Mississippi. While there I started teaching a night class on base for the University of Mississippi, from which I had received my Masters Degree in English. In January, I also took a full time job teaching junior and senior English for the Back Bay Biloxi High School. In August of 1969, we moved to San Antonio, Texas for a two and one half year tour. In January of 1970 I got a teaching job with Northside ISD at John Jay High School as a replacement eleventh grade English teacher for a young woman who was obviously pregnant and therefore at that time was not allowed to continue teaching while pregnant. By the end of the semester, I also was pregnant, carrying our first child, so I had to give up teaching for a while. As our family continued to grow, I did not teach full time again until 1980 when we had returned to San Antonio for Joel's final assignment before retiring from the Air Force. During the following eighteen years, I taught all English grades plus Creative Writing at John Jay High School. I received special joy in sponsoring the school literary magazine, Parnassus, every year. The students and I took such pride in its production. Later, at Communications Arts High School, I began an NISD poetry writing contest each year which was named the May Day Poetry Competition, and was celebrated on a special night in May to honor the district-wide winners. Students and parents alike really appreciated such attention being paid to literary achievement, and the contest continued for many years after my retirement.

In 1984, I had received the opportunity to attend a summer institute conducted by the National Writing Project, held at Trinity University. That proved to be the beginning of years of interest in improving my own writing skills and my ability to help my students improve their individual writing skills. In the summer of 1985, I attended an NISD writing institute conducted by Dr. Joyce Armstrong Carroll and her husband, Eddie Wilson, their own spinoff of the National Project which they named the New Jersey Writing Project in Texas. Those two summers made such a difference in my own teaching as well as for many other teachers. Joyce 'n' Eddie later renamed their project the Abydos Writing Project, and they made a significant impact on the teaching of writing in Texas schools. I personally felt my teaching and writing skills were greatly improved through that training. I became a writing trainer myself in 1991 and even taught an institute in Florida during the summer of 1993.

``Also, during those years I taught college level night classes for San Antonio College, Palo Alto College, Northwest Vista College, and University of Texas at San Antonio. I loved teaching literature and writing skills, but I eventually began to realize that my greatest interest lay in the writing of poetry, which is apparent in the writing of this memoir. I started a poetry writing competition for NISD high school students called the May Day Poetry Contest which continued for many years and helped students receive encouragement and acclaim for their poetic efforts. Also, I assisted in conducting a nationwide poetry contest for adults with a publication of winning poems called Poetry Along the River. I truly enjoyed all this involvement because poetry, for me, captures and preserves life more beautifully and precisely than any other format, though all writing forms have their indisputable worth. I have, for years, participated in poetry groups and a book club, and I have attended many literary presentations of all types - all contributing to my growth and benefit. I hope that the time never comes when I am no longer learning and growing, mentally and emotionally. Words preserve us, and beautifully composed words preserve us more memorably.

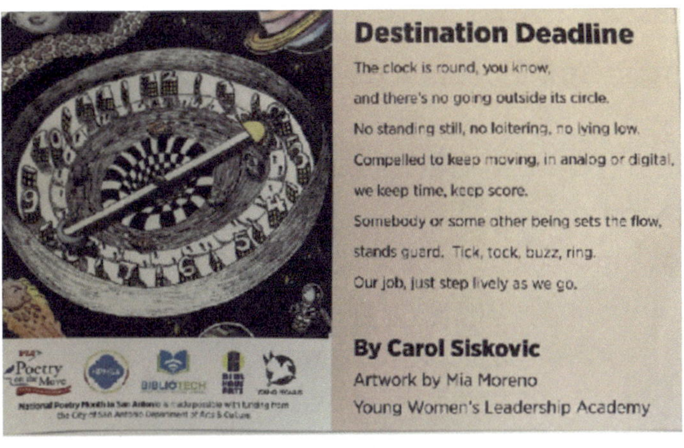

A Winner of the VIA San Antonio's POETRY ON THE MOVE Contest. Posted on all San Antonio VIA buses for a full year.

Books and Poems - Hold On

Like Mom and Dad and Grands,
or memories of bliss,
like blue skies and massive spans,
or a lover's long sweet kiss…
the words of our brains caress,
implant, and wind their way,
connect, affect, impress,
and latch on tight to stay.

Carol M. Siskovic

Destination Deadline

The clock is round, you know,
and there's no going outside its circle.
No standing still, no loitering, no lying low.
Compelled to keep moving, in analog or digital,
we keep time, keep score.
Somebody or some other being sets the flow,
stands guard. Tick, tock, buzz, ring.
Our job, just step lively as we go.

Carol M. Siskovic
(A winning poem in
San Antonio Poetry on the Move contest,
posted on city buses for the year)

Another Step Forward

A clean desk, toys of play entice.
A globe displays places not yet seen;
window scenes show change of season,
things to do, chances to take.
A world awaits.

So many stages, graduations, possibilities!
How sweet and how terrifying this life!
Choices like the stars fill our endless sky.
Life beckons, tempts, dares, thrills!
Even quiet lulls, leads us forward.

The past taught, still teaches.
The Next calls ……………..

Carol M. Siskovic

Monologue-mania

Listen to me! Listen to me, I say. To all my "ations."
Tribulations…meditations...lamentations...
condemnations…contemplations...celebrations...
augmentations…assignations...argumentations.
My emptying, and your small, if temporary, recognitions
provide the only libation, that long-lusted verification.
Underneath, please see the layers and layers.
Black and white shifts of priceless lace, colorful silks,
sturdy weaves, at least one top hat or fascinator,
snug wraps, cloaks, tap shoes, toe shoes, no shoes.
Top to bottom, rings of spiraling rings,
breezes ever blowing gentle but strong enough
to carry you elsewhere even as your heart
takes root along-side mine.

Carol M. Siskovic

Creative Slam

I want words to bombard my brain
and then magically sort into streams of beauty,
rivers of intellectual insight and oceans of endless truth.
I want to write something worthy-
that is easily recognized for its wisdom
and loveliness and usefulness to all humankind.
That is my desire and if I can do it for me alone
or just for my own children,
then my life has special meaning.
If somehow, a book of mine or a single work could live on,
my life will be fulfilled.

Carol M. Siskovic

Confidentially

My mind is ajar
Flies rumble within
Birds roost in my attic
Mice run in my maze

Green things romp wildly
Grow like wet vines
Hoards of thin string
Loop and entwine

No doorbell to ring
No knocker to knock
A rock wriggling with worms
Where scorpions lie hid

My mind is ajar
Now screw on the lid!

Carol M. Siskovic

What a Poem Is Not

Not a proof of intelligence or talent.
Not a guarantee of longevity or loveliness.

No insurance of ease in writing, understanding,
No definite connection with all, or anyone else.
No assurance of a sense of completion.

Never a waste of time, no matter who judges.
Never lacking a degree of catharsis.
Never without vibrations of enjoyment, satisfaction.
Never never ever less than a child born of the heart.

As a moth drawn to hot light, a poem must
do what it does, be what it is; it cannot seek safety.
It wants to please, but it never depends on approval.
It cannot become for praise or reward.
The saddest negative is a poem felt, but not written.

Carol M. Siskovic

Weddings…Weddings

22

As the years went by and the kids grew up, there were so many stories and so many memories culminating in their four marriages. None of them rushed out to get married right away. The first marriage was Cara's in 1997. Cara would graduate from college in December 1996, and early that year she had met Frank Latt, a Marine pilot. They had decided that they were meant for each other so they planned a January 1997 marriage, and it was going to be a "Big Ta-do." We arranged for them to use the club at Randolph Air Force Base, to get rooms on base for all the people who would be out-of-town attendees, and for the marriage to take place in the church there. The reception was to be at the club on base. Everything worked out perfectly, and it was a beautiful and wonderful affair. After the wedding ceremony, the attendees waited outside the church for the bride and groom to exit the church together, walking beneath an arch of swords that marines were holding. At the end of the arch, Cara, and all of us in the watching crowd, were surprised and astonished by a slap of the last sword against her rear with the resounding shout of "Welcome to the Marine Corp, Ma'am!" It was an unexpected occurrence for most of the crowd, especially the Bride, who jumped and screeched! To say the least! Everybody laughed and laughed! Then it was off to the club for a lovely reception and dance.

The next marriage was in 2006, and that was Holly's wedding to Brian Ballew. She and Brian had met at Community Bible Church, in northeast San Antonio. We had attended some services there, and Holly decided to attend the adult singles Sunday School class. She met Brian there, and they began to date. They were soon engaged, and got married January 7 at our nearby Baptist church on Wurzbach that she had attended for a few years. We had the wedding in the church and the reception in the church reception hall. It was lovely, and they came back to our house right after the wedding, opened more presents and spent some time with everyone in the family for a while before everyone from out of state had to return home.. Then, Holly and Brian went off on a special honeymoon cruise around the Virgin Islands. They both owned houses in San Antonio so they had to decide which to sell, then get themselves settled in the other to begin their married life together.

The next year, in 2007, Jeannie got married on May 27, and Lee got married on September 8. Jeannie's wedding was the only one that did not occur in San Antonio. She and her future husband, Matt Salo, were going to make Alexandria, Virginia, their permanent address as they both had jobs and careers in the DC area. They had come to know each other through their after-work gatherings in some downtown DC favored relaxing spots where unattached DC workers usually met. After the honeymoon, they planned to live in the home that Matt already owned. They still live there now, after putting it through several renovations.

They chose to get married outside DC in the countryside in a vineyard in Virginia. They had spent memorable weekend moments in that area while dating. After a perfect pre-wedding dinner nearby, just before time for the outdoor wedding, Jeannie became upset and worried because there was a real possibility of rain coming. Luckily, she didn't hear until later that her wedding ring was dropped down the sink in the men's room right before the wedding started and had to be rescued just in time. Ironically, I had written the perfect poem which I read just before their vows. As I read aloud, lightning flashed in the background. Everything had gone beautifully, but the sky flashed signals, and then it did start to sprinkle just before they said "I do." With those words, the whole wedding party got up and ran for the covered dining area. Once everyone got under cover and somewhat settled there, the pastor made the final pronouncement of "man and wife." The rest of the evening included partying, dancing, and fun together time.

Cara and Frank, at that time, were stationed near the Pentagon and lived in their townhouse nearby so we stayed with them after the wedding for a few days and then came home and began to prepare ourselves for Lee's September wedding in San Antonio.

Lee and Deb Ireland were getting married at the top of a somewhat historic tall building in the area close to Trinity University. That was practically an outside wedding, too, in that the ceremony took place on the roof of the building in a quite memorable and beautiful location overlooking the city. It was common at dusk for a flock of birds to come flying into a nearby chimney opening, seeking their shelter for the night, and those of us who knew that were hoping for such a sight on this occasion. But the crowd must have been too frightening or the time a little too long before dark, since the ceremony was concluded without a bird in sight. The reception was on the floor below the roof so as the ceremony ended, we all departed for food and fun. When the party ended and everybody left, the couple actually had an apartment at the back of the reception room. They spent their wedding night there, had late night snacks on the roof with a beautiful view of the city and could wake up and have breakfast on the rooftop, which all made for a truly memorable occasion. Now, all our children were married. And our first grandchild, two-year-old Frankie Latt, had attended the last two of the weddings. Also, at the last wedding, Holly was pretty sure that another grandchild was on the way. She didn't dream that it would be twin boys.

Cara and Frank Latt

Holly and Brian Ballew

Jeannie and Matt Sala

Joel "Lee" and Deb Siskovic

Pledging Myself with This Vow, I DO

I grasp your same promise,
merge it with my own,
as we begin our "together life"
on this happy wedding day,

TOGETHER!
Such a lovely concept,
one that can build and grow,
adding daily to our dream,
our happiness, our hope.

At special times, maybe every day,
we will remember, renew this blending.
Two lives melding together
with those precious words
   spoken from the heart and soul:
      "I do!" "We do!"

Carol M. Siskovic

Wedding Day

Somewhere, perhaps in cons past
A part of you and a part of me
Blew into being from God's own breath.

Generations of becoming
Brought us here this day to clasp together
Hands and hearts and happiness,

To pledge our troth, our truth,
Undying faithfulness as one.
I marry you. I marry you. I marry you.

Feel the fastening of our Selves,
Miracle of miracles, two strengths
Remaining two, yet melding daily into one.

Oh, blessed love! Oh, blessed day!
When centuries thunder to this
Pronouncement beautiful.

I do.   I do.
Now, watch love's lightning
Write **WE** across our lives.

Vows and invocations roll like raindrops
Into the river of Commitment,
Flowing to the sea of Unity,
The ocean of Reinvention.

Carol M. Siskovic

The Essentials

Begin with wine,
a million toasts.
Salute the moment, the day,
each week, month, year.
Drink to each other
with eyes of love,
sometimes with water only
sometimes the strongest of spirits.

You are the salt.
Each of you flavor the blandness
and preserve each other
against the archenemy, Sorrow
and the combatant. Trouble.
Savor the identifiable taste
of your togetherness,
your together purpose.

Seek the deep, dark sweetness
unlike any other yet known,
the comfort as satisfying
as expensive chocolate,
the joy of embraces
which stir bitterness
into melted mellowness,
leaving you strengthened.

Learn to wield a broom
against dust and leaves,
trash and debris
that block the heart passages.
Sweep away, sweep away
all that harms,
all that eats at
the sanctity of love.

Prepare and take bread daily,
at the same table in unity.
Feed each other
with your own hands.
Ensure each other's health,
growth, and well-being.
For if you exist happily,
your bond is your bread.

May you end
as you begin,
with a well-blended wine,
toasting a full life,
a happy home,
a bond well-made,
and a long, long life for
two who chose to become One.

Carol M. Siskovic

A Rescue

23

With our children all married and scattered about in different states, Joel and
I devoted ourselves to traveling about and enjoying ourselves. Joel had dreamed of camping activities for a long time. I had first realized that when he had come home with a sudden purchase while we were living in Bowie, Maryland, in 1974. He was so happy to show off his perfect find, a 1970 Volkswagen camper. Then he also found a place that would install a lift-up top so that we would have more sleeping room for the kids. We camped all over during our four years in England and later in the states, so it was only natural that he would want to get more serious about camping now that we were retired and on our own again. I should not have been surprised at all when on a Sunday afternoon drive with friends through the small town of Comfort, Texas, Joel suddenly yelled, "Stop! Go back!" He had spied a large camper with a "For Sale" sign posted on it.

It turned out to be a 1976 RV that was extremely reasonable. It turned out to also need a lot of work and renovation, but that was part of the fun for him. He soon located a camping group which we joined, and it became a joke that we always seemed to have some automotive trouble that required us to call for help. So much so that Joel build a friendship with James Brown, a mechanic who always seemed to be available to come to our rescue. Our fellow campers, to this day, recall the many times James Brown came to our rescue, once when we had come to a dead standstill on a turning lane off Highway I -10!

For many years we camped and enjoyed our outings. But it all came to an end in 2016. We had gone to Sam's Club to buy a replacement house battery and were heading home. I was doing all the driving by that time because of Joel's failed eyesight, and I had started to pull out into the back street when Joel again yelled "STOP!" This time was far more urgent. He had spotted a curl of smoke coming from the engine which was located right between the two front seats.

What we did not know was that the gasoline had been slowly eating away at the gas line, and it had finally sprung a leak. I hit the brakes and the motor died. He said "Smoke...," and I looked at the motor. Small curled smoke drifted up from there, and he jumped up and grabbed the fire extinguisher. When he lifted the top off of the motor to spray the extinguisher, that little smoke curl turned into a tiny little flame. He started spraying, but it didn't help, and all of a sudden the small flame became a huge blaze. He was thrown back, and everything started burning so fast. I was strapped in my seatbelt, which made it difficult to get loose. He had fallen back on the floor, and I was trying to get away from the flame. It was just unimaginably huge, going up to the ceiling and already burning the bed that was above the two front passenger seats. Everything was black, and the smoke was so thick and awful. I kept trying to get loose, but I couldn't see. My right hand got burned in the flame trying to get the safety belt off, but finally I got free and lunged toward the walkway into Joel, both of us falling to the floor.

My arm was burned. My face was burned, and as I had gone through the fire, I had burned my stomach area too. I was trying to get up off the floor. It had been difficult to get out of that front seat anyway, and I had hurled myself backwards as soon as I was free. Joel had been trying to get to me, but I hadn't been able see him. I didn't know he was there because the smoke was so thick. I rammed right into him, and both of us were struggling on the floor. He crawled and tried to open the RV door with no success as everything became pitch-black and unbreathable. I was saying, “Can you get the door open?” and he muttered, “I'm trying, I'm trying.”

I was finding at that time that I didn't have the energy or the breath to get up. And I remember realizing, “This is it. I never knew it would happen like this. I can't believe it.” I felt I was about to pass out. Then, all of a sudden, the door opened. And there was a young man, saying, “Sir, can I help you get out?” He helped him as Joel crawled, and finally, he got him out, and somebody else was there to grab him. Then the young voice asked, “Is there anybody else?" and Joel was choking. He coughed, “My wife” and a voice asked, “Ma'am Ma'am, are you in there?” I was barely able to gasp, “Yes. Yes.” He said, “Can you stand up?” And I could hardly say “no.” But I did and he said, “Can you crawl over to me?” I crawled over as well as I could, and he said, “Can you stand up now?” I couldn't, so he

helped me crawl down the steps down to the concrete. Then he put his arms around my waist and helped me crawl away from the RV and up the hill toward a tree. There were some women there who had run over to assist. They helped me stand up at the tree, and then they helped me go over to the corner of a building. Then I turned around and looked. He had run back to see if Joel had been taken care of. All of a sudden, the tires started popping and there were huge explosions. The fire was all over the bus and the light pole at the corner. All of that happened within a few minutes, and the whole bus was now burning. If we had been in the RV at that time, we definitely would have been killed. We had to be hospitalized and receive treatment for our burns and oxygen deprivation, but we recovered within a few weeks. We learned that the young man who saved us was Anthony Beverly. He had gone to school at John Jay High School where I had taught for 18 years, and he had been going there when I first started teaching there in 1980. I never taught him, but I remembered him because he was a well known football player who had received a scholarship to SMU. We later found out that he now lived only a short way from us, right in our neighborhood. We had not known him, and he had saved our lives that day.

I had five years left with Joel because of this rescue. And I myself have had more than five additional years of life due to Anthony's heroic run from his car to a burning RV. From that point on, Joel and I tried to be sure to appreciate every moment of life. We lived each day with a new zeal and gratefulness. That was truly a gift that came from our near tragedy, though we definitely regretted the loss of our old blue and white '76 RV, with its treasure trove of memories.

Our rescuer, Anthony Beverly was a former John Jay HS and SMU student, and also happened to live only a few streets from us. He was named Outstanding Northside ISD Alumni for 2016.

The Mind, The Soul, The You

I gaze so often upon this beautiful view,
watching the play of ocean waves upon the sand.
I am reminded of a child playing with toy figures,
providing the conversation, the plot, the intrigue.
Then losing interest in the repetitiveness.
Leaving, but always returning for the solace.

How can it be that part of you remains,
and so much has long ago sailed into the vastness?
I think I see a wave-tip of recognition, a splash.
Then, the glint mixes with sand and flows away.
My heart tries to follow, imagine your watery view.
Understand the terrible, yet peaceful, betweenness.

Some days I wonder how it would be to catch the waves,
wash far far out, at last part of that eternal movement,
part of constant change, unending reformation.
Other days, I side with the sand, struggling to hang on,
hold a little longer to the known, what seems more secure.
I can almost hear the rocks sneering in their own struggle.

Truth with its multiple facets pulls, releases, just as my love
holds to you against the relentless tug of Time's ocean.
Science talks of capturing mind and memories,
placing them in a robotic, undying body, but
you and I know deep down each day,
the rhythmic pounding of goodby.

Carol M. Siskovic (January 25, 2020)

Pay Attention!

Today's sun is all there is, here, today.
Shadowy or glaring, the world outside
these windows is a first world, first seen,
like this, like this, like this, like this.
This moment, this sight, just right
for this glance, this trance, as I
glide through this piece of time.

Let a poem begin.
It hovers hungry
to consume someone's,
everyone's attention,
to whisper or yell.
In a perked or half-listening
place we call mindfulness,
this, this combination
of sounds can give
guidance or entertainment,
show a path leading
where you would not have gone,
or if you had,
would never have noticed,
much less absorbed
into who and what you are.
Each moment offers choice:
To sink into this bed of words,
to store them, to ignore them,
or to act upon them,
use them.

Carol M. Siskovic

Last Day Together

24

How many times in history have people said, "If only we had known…?" When I think back on that morning, it seems like so many similar mornings we spent together: waking, dressing, eating breakfast while sitting in our LazyBoy chairs as we watched/listened to TV, making or taking phone calls, then a quick lunch before getting ready for another appointment for Joel, getting him on his scooter and out to the car, loading him in the car, driving the scooter to its lift for attachment, then heading out to the clinic for a treatment. All of these "together" activities for the last time. Joel had been fighting physical problems for years. During the Vietnam War and especially during that horrible TET attack in 1968, he had been exposed to Agent Orange and numerous other smoke exposures. He had been fighting PTSD and diabetes for years, plus other varying ailments. He had lost a lot of his sight, and he had to use a wheelchair full-time. So, after a lot of research, he had decided that his condition could be improved by a series of O3 infusions. This day was to be his third.

So funny that our last conversation was an argument. His treatment finished, he was preparing to leave, and a couple of nurses were still standing about. Also, there was David Neison, a good friend of Joel's who had been there for a treatment of his own, another patient I didn't know, and the lady who ran the clinic. It was a group of about seven of us, all talking and laughing. Then somebody asked Joel why he was going through this set of five blood transfers. He glanced at me, then said, "Because I want to live as long as I can. I know I'm going first, but I want to be here for Carol as long as I can." I had heard him say that so many times, but for some reason, this time it bothered me. I replied, "You have absolutely no idea which of us will be going first! I could drop dead at any time! That's not a thing any of us can know!" Then I noticed everyone was smiling, and Joel and I started smiling too.

But still, he persisted, "I know, and that's why I'm doing all I can to last as long as I can." Of course, I persisted with some curt remark, saying he couldn't be sure and walked out ahead of him to prepare his lift for leaving. He followed shortly, and I had to help him a little as he struggled to push himself up into his car seat while saying, "Get me home." Then I drove his scooter onto the lift and raised it. As I got in the car and began to crank up, Joel said again with some urgency, "Get me home." Pulling out onto the street, I told him, "I'm really tired today, too. Definitely ready to go home." As I drove, I looked over at him as his chin dropped onto his chest. I said, "Joel, are you going to sleep?!!" Another look, and I realized he had passed out. With a quick signal, I did a u-turn and pulled back in front of the clinic, blowing my horn like crazy. Three staff members raced out, one of them bringing oxygen. They did all they could as one called EMS. Joel, without opening his eyes or raising his head, said one last time, "Get me home," then went unconscious. At that time I called my son-in-law, Brian Ballew, the only one in town as he had not gone on a beach vacation with the rest of the family. The EMS staff arrived and worked with Joel, putting him in their vehicle, a difficult maneuver to say the least.

Then, after not allowing me in with Joel, finally the driver came out and told me to follow them to Methodist Emergency, nearby but still a long, agonizing journey. I had to park in the huge parking building next door, then walk in and wait in line before finally being escorted to the area where they had taken Joel. I could tell from the attendant's behavior that things were not good. When I went in, a group of doctors and nurses surrounded Joel, not doing anything. They stepped aside to allow me next to him, and the main doctor looked at me and quietly asked, "Are you ready for me to call it?" Ready or not, it was obviously a fact, so I nodded
as I clutched Joel's arm. It was clear they had really tried hard to revive him, with no success. At that very moment, I received a call from my daughter Jeannie asking for an update, and I was able to tell her, crying, that their Dad had passed. The very understanding group of medical professionals, all but one who kept a distant watch, quietly left me to say my goodbyes.

I was soon joined by my son-in-law, Brian Ballew, who quietly stayed with me for the next hour or so until Joel's body was picked up by Neptune, the group we had an arrangement with for cremation. All the other children who were together for vacation at Rehoboth Beach, Delaware, now had received word, and all the children were quickly making arrangements to get home, all traveling through the night and arriving early the next day. From the hospital, Brian escorted me home where Ana Torres (who after working for me for years had become like another daughter to me) was waiting to grieve with me and stay with me until the family could get there.

Jocl must have been so proud of how the family came together, supporting each other, and preparing a truly fitting and wonderful memorial service for August 14, 2021 — the day after Joel would have celebrated his 81st birthday on August 13. Many attended and commented on how perfect the service was, celebrating Joel's life and his positive effect on everyone who knew him. His ashes were placed in Columbarium Three at Fort Sam Houston where mine will one day join his. Just a reminder of how joyful and satisfying two lives melded can be. Until then, he's always with us. Not gone. Never forgotten. Still guiding and inspiring his family.

Our Love's Sweet Flight
A Golden Anniversary

Fifty years is n'er enough
for such rare-feathered birds as us.
We mated young and innocent
and all these golden years have spent
like bookends, never very far apart,
almost one mind, almost one heart.
Give us a decade or a century more,
we'll soar together as we have before,
through darkened shadow to mountain crest,
aloft, then warm within our nest.
We're soul-united, side by side ...
this life, the next, our love abides.

Carol M. Siskovic

(Written for all couples fortunate enough to
spend a half century together.
Joel and I celebrated 54 years together on
May 6, 2021, before he passed on August 5, 2021)

Passing it On

25

This book is just a small effort to pass on some memorable stories of my life that might be lost forever with my passing. In making this attempt to capture and save memories, I have come to several realizations.

1. During the busy discovery times of youth, we usually are so involved in learning and living our own lives that we take little interest in the stories of other lives. I look back and regret that I asked so few questions of my family members who are now passed on. I also regret that they left no writings of accounts or explanations. As a result I have very little information to pass on about the Malone, Vanlandingham, Horton and Ramay families. Nothing written by ancestors, few pictures. Joel was left even less by the Siskovic, Pirhalla, and Barbuschak families on his side. With access to so many modern means, I am hoping that my children and their families will leave much much more information for their future generations to learn from, descriptions of their problems, difficulties, accomplishments, pleasures, desires, beliefs, loves, fears, hopes.

2. There is no way in telling the past to capture absolute accuracy or to be certain of how your telling will be received, of how your telling may affect future kin. One thing for sure is that silence has no effect; or perhaps that absence and lack is the effect.

3. There is no point at which you have finally shared everything exactly as you would like it told. There is only what you decide is the stopping point - for now. Perhaps there will be time for more. Perhaps not. A good friend of mine just died, suddenly. No time for the questions or discussions we thought we would eventually get around to.

No time left to “catch up,” as we often promised we would get to… soon.

4. We all seem to be avid collectors as we live our lives, saving so many ‘things” that we can’t keep up with them ourselves. Plus, the longer we live, the more likely we are to forget, even many of those things we would have sworn we could never forget. So, again, we need to be more vigilant: in ridding ourselves of the unimportant, no longer useful or valuable belongings; and in writing down or recording in some modern manner the history and value of what’s being passed on.

5. “Words, words, words,” as Shakespeare wrote so long ago, can mean so much or so little, but absence of words only leaves room for presumption.

I want to declare emphatically to my family and friends, to each individually and personally: “I LOVE YOU BEYOND WORDS, AND ETERNALLY! PASS IT ON!”

A Place

I try to plant my feet
in this land of words,
search out corners
and closets,
but I feel myself floating
and flying unanchored,
chasing filaments of thought,
mists of meaning.
If, if only, I could
scoop and capture,
arrange on a string,
stack in a pack,
stir, whir, mix, fix,
I'd have a concoction,
a kite, a continuance,
all mine but also yours,
and everyone's,
for now and later,
useful and joyful,
simply because I came here
to this place of poetry,
listened between the flutters
and the flairs, then closed
my being around a poem.

Carol M. Siskovic

Family Photos 2023

Acknowledgments

Without the lifelong support and influence of so many family members, I would have little reason or compulsion to record anything for posterity. So I want to put in writing my deep thankfulness to all those, living and passed on, who have helped make me who and what I am. In the present age, so many families seem to be disjointed, unforgiving, and unsupportive that I feel extremely fortunate to have experienced the opposite. Even though I no longer see many of those relatives very much, their influence remains constant. My immediate family in its closeness and devotion proves a result and reflection of those past family strengths and connections. It is my wish that even though future generations may live farther distances apart that modern communication devices will allow and encourage lifelong constant connection, that we remain consciously intertwined.

Special thanks must go to my oldest daughter, Holly Siskovic Ballew, for her undaunting support and encouragement. It was she who began recording my frequent meandering life stories and transposing them into print. It was she who encouraged me to visualize a completed book containing pictures and poems to accompany my recollections. She has served as a diligent and determined editor. She foresaw a finished product and has worked to bring it to fruition, especially for the benefit of our family, but also convinced that many others will find value or enjoyment, perhaps both, in the reading of this collection of one person's life stories.

I especially thank Beth who allowed me to be helpful in the completion of her own book, Where the Waters Take Us, She also provided us with much needed information about publishing as well as the use of her publishing company, Basking Turtle, which fits perfectly our Siskovic "Turtles" family.

An advanced thank you I send forward to all future readers, perhaps some who are not born yet. How we choose to spend our time is so important, and I truly hope that my writings will have informed, entertained, perhaps inspired. Maybe even encouraged you to record your own life stories for your descendants.

Made in the USA
Columbia, SC
09 February 2025